ETHICAL ASPECTS
OF
TRAGEDY

ETHICAL ASPECTS
OF
TRAGEDY

A Comparison
of Certain Tragedies
by
Aeschylus, Sophocles, Euripides, Seneca
and
Shakespeare

by
LAURA JEPSEN

AMS PRESS
NEW YORK

Reprinted by arrangement with the author from the edition of 1953, Gainesville
First AMS edition published 1971

Manufactured in the United States of America

International Standard Book Number: 0-404-03566-3

Library of Congress Number: 79-153332

AMS PRESS INC.
NEW YORK, N.Y. 10003

PREFACE

A SMALL BOOK on so large a subject as Greek, Roman, and English tragedy needs some justification, especially since volumes have been written about single aspects of each play. However, Aristotle's *Poetics* is brief, and this book is, in part, an effort to augment the lecture notes of the hypothetical student to whom we are indebted for the fragments of Aristotle's treatise. In part, it is an effort to determine in how far Aristotle's idea of *ethos* is applicable to various tragedies of Aeschylus, Sophocles, Euripides, Seneca, and Shakespeare.

In this study I have analyzed only plays of generally admitted tragic power, and have attempted by direct attention to the works themselves to interpret the authors concerned. That is not to pretend that a play springs from a definite concept of tragedy held by the author, but it is to maintain that a particular work of an author is informed by a certain viewpoint, whether consciously or unconsciously expressed, and that that viewpoint may be defined in a theory of tragedy. Since in this book all theories are deduced from the idea of *ethos*, I have called the book not *Theories of Tragedy* but *Ethical Aspects of Tragedy*.

The method is one of analogy, in which comparisons are drawn between pairs of classical and Shakespearean tragedies. However, it should be emphasized that absolute parallels they are not, and I have no desire to stress chance likenesses. Moreover, between various aspects of *ethos* there is a narrow line of demarcation, and several aspects may be found in a single tragedy. Thus, pathos and stoicism may appear in a tragedy which culminates in poetic justice, and irony of some kind may be all-pervasive. Nevertheless, it should be said that in every instance the resolution of the tragedy is clear and may be expressed as a distinct aspect of *ethos*.

Briefly expressing the "idea of tragedy" emphasized by the three Greek tragedians and Shakespeare, William Chase Greene in his book *Moira* summarizes the several modes of tragedy relating most aptly to *ethos*. Greene writes, "Aeschylus has boldly adapted the myths in order to exhibit the increasing justice of Zeus." This is the aspect called elsewhere by Greene "poetic justice." But in the tragedies of Sophocles, Euripides, and Shakespeare Greene finds a pervading irony. He discovers, "Blind destiny is supplanted for Sophocles by irony, the spectacle of man's blindness or ignorance of whatever truth is unknown to him. For Euripides, sceptical of the myths, if not of religion, *pathos,* the tragic sense, will be the last resort of the poet; he thus marks a return to the earliest phase of tragedy, while experimenting with the moral ideas of his day in the spirit of the sophists and of Thucydides. Shakespeare's tragedies arouse in us a sense of the pitiful waste of human excellence in a world which neither protects nor persecutes nobility but lets it fall, now (like Cordelia) through the operation of some evil force or some mischance, now like Hamlet, or Othello, through the terrible and unexpected recoil of well-meaning efforts. This is not fatalism, but once more a sense of the ironical."

Finally, in the decay of the ancient world, the Roman Seneca, interested still in the problem of *ethos* but remote from the spirit of irony, found consolation in Stoicism. By accepting the universe, by making its law his law, the

Stoic could find happiness, or failing in his quest for happiness he could by his ultimate resignation at least find peace in death.

A few words should be said about the plan of the book. After an initial chapter defining the idea of *ethos* in the Aristotelian sense, a chapter is devoted to each aspect of *ethos*. The discussion depends on philosophic analyses, not on chronological relationship; but anyone who notes the dates of the classical authors will observe that their works follow a time sequence and serve as a standard of comparison for the Shakespearean tragedies.

I have tried not to encumber my text or notes with controversy, though I have occasionally observed disagreement. My chief concern in documentation has been to indicate points at which my conclusions are expressed or implied by other critics. In the course of this undertaking I have profited by reading a number of books by various authors, although I have included in the notes only those works which seemed to me most valuable in this study.

I am aware that I may be censured by those who feel that I have paid too little attention to aspects of tragedy unrelated to my subject, to what Aristotle might call diction, thought, song, or spectacle. If I have done this, I have done it deliberately, because it seemed to me that the ethical aspects of tragedy have been too long neglected. To study the element of *ethos* as it contributes to the greatness of tragedy is the purpose of this book. If these essays, limited in scope, send the reader back to the plays with fresh insight, they have fulfilled their purpose.

L. J.

Tallahassee, Florida

CONTENTS

ONE — *ETHOS* IN TRAGEDY *1*

TWO — POETIC JUSTICE *8*

Aeschylus   THE ORESTEIA

Shakespeare   MACBETH

THREE — POETIC IRONY *32*

Sophocles   OEDIPUS THE KING   *Shakespeare*   OTHELLO
              OEDIPUS AT COLONUS   KING LEAR
              ANTIGONE   HAMLET

FOUR — PATHOS *75*

Euripides   HIPPOLYTUS

Shakespeare   ROMEO AND JULIET

FIVE — ROMANTIC IRONY *88*

Euripides   THE BACCHAE

Shakespeare   ANTONY AND CLEOPATRA

SIX — STOICISM *102*

Seneca   HERCULES OETAEUS

Shakespeare   JULIUS CAESAR

NOTES *117*

INDEX *127*

ix

ETHOS IN TRAGEDY

ARISTOTLE came at an opportune time, after the tragedians of the fifth century had done their work, and thus had at his disposal a vast repository of Greek drama, much of which is no longer extant. After studying that body of literature, Aristotle, speaking with his "notorious and habitual" importance, formulated a definition and fixed tragedy in a conventional form or genre.

The fact that Aristotle's *Poetics* reached us in what seems to be a series of lecture notes has permitted critics wide opportunity for speculation. Nevertheless, from this fragmentary document certain conclusions can be drawn and certain aspects of *ethos* in tragedy inferred.

Aristotle was essentially interested in studying the development of tragedy as it approached its natural limits or as it achieved its ideal potentialities. "Having passed through many changes, it found its natural form, and there it stopped," Aristotle affirms in the *Poetics*.[1] It attained its ideal, according to Aristotle, in the works of Sophocles and Euripides; indeed, Aristotle derives from certain of their tragedies most of the criteria for his conception of ideal tragedy. Dryden once affirmed, "It is not enough that Aristotle has said so, for Aristotle drew his models of tragedy from Sophocles and Euripides; and if he had seen ours, might have changed his mind."[2] Though one can hardly claim omniscience for Aristotle, it would seem that Dryden is wrong, and that Aristotle, if he had seen ours, would still have believed that beyond the Sophoclean idea of tragedy there could be no further development.

Ethos, a concept important to an understanding of Aristotelian thought, is summarily touched upon in the *Poetics* and further dealt with in the *Nicomachean Ethics* and in the *Rhetoric*. *Ethos* is here used as Aristotle uses it, to refer to the moral character of an initially good man, a character derived from action based upon moral choice, whether that choice appear ultimately as good or bad. In this book the concept will be examined not only in the light of Aristotle's analysis but also in its wider significance, as it informs classical and Shakespearean tragedy.

Regarded from the point of view of the audience in the theater, who must feel sympathy with the sufferer in order to appreciate the tragedy, *ethos* is the most significant of Aristotle's six essentials of tragedy; for it is *ethos* in action —or action with an ethical import—which evokes the emotions of pity and fear, which give rise to what Aristotle calls the pleasure proper to tragedy. Butcher, in his comments on Aristotle's theory, lucidly emphasizes the need of a predominantly good hero to create the pleasure arising, paradoxically, from pain in witnessing the spectacle of tragic suffering: "The qualities requisite to such a character are here deduced from the primary fact that the function of tragedy is to produce the *katharsis* of pity and fear; pity being felt for a person who, if not wholly innocent, meets with suffering beyond his deserts; fear being awakened when the sufferer is a man of like nature with ourselves. Tragic character must be exhibited through the medium of a plot which has the capacity of giving full satisfaction to these emotions. Certain types, therefore, of character and

2

certain forms of catastrophe are at once excluded, as failing either in whole or in part to produce the tragic effect."[3]

The reciprocal relation of character and action—of action produced by character and character issuing in action—is emphasized by Aristotle. But since tragic characters assume *ethos* on the basis of their actions, Aristotle quite logically insists, "Plot, then, is the first principle, and, as it were, the soul of a tragedy: Character holds the second place."[4] Even a drama like Agathon's *Anthus*, though it evidently manifested *ethos* of the simplest kind only,[5] might be called a tragedy because it presented action. Stressing the significance of character, Aristotle affirms, "The tragedies of most of our modern poets fail in the rendering of character; and of poets in general this is often true."[6] In analyzing the essentials of character, the author of the *Poetics* says, "First, and most important, it must be good. Now any speech or action that manifests moral purpose of any kind will be expressive of character: the character will be good if the purpose is good."[7]

Nineteenth-century critics have been accused of stressing "character" at the expense of action in the plays of Shakespeare, and subsequently of seeking a moral in a play, contrary to the author's intent. Aristotle, too, would most likely have frowned upon such practice, for his doctrine of ethics is subsidiary to, though indispensable for, his esthetic dictum. In other words, for Aristotle the ethical sense is basic to the esthetic power of tragedy; there is no dichotomy in *utile dulci;* such distinction was a later discovery, by Horace.

Aristotle is interested in the protagonist primarily as a good character,[8] one who observes the moral laws of the universe. However, the ideal hero cannot be wholly good; he must have some *hamartia*, some fault or flaw, which to the Greek mind was frequently associated with violation of the doctrine of "the mean." It is a common observation that the Greeks of the classical period had no idea of evil such as the English word *sin* connotes, that is, violation of some sacred command of a deity, or adherence to the ways of the Devil rather than the words of God. Rather, they conceived of vice as a disturbance of a balanced proportion in the universe or as a failure to hit the target at the exact point representing virtue. Nor was vice, according to the doctrine of the mean, at the opposite pole from virtue. Aristotle defines moral virtue as a "mean state between two vices, one of excess and one of defect." The mean is a good relative to the extremes on either side; and as a moral good, it is an extreme. Aristotle qualifies his remark with the statement, "Virtue then is a settled disposition of the mind determining the choice of actions and emotions, consisting essentially in the observance of the mean relative to us, this being determined by principle, that is, as the prudent man would determine it."[9] Even the idea of *hybris* punished by nemesis—the idea of pride going before a fall—is founded on the notion of excess, or deviation from the mean relative to us.

Of the difficulty of observing the mean, Aristotle is fully aware, for he gives certain precautions that will best enable a man to "hit the mean," and then adds: "But no doubt it is a difficult thing to do, and especially in particular cases: for instance, it is not easy to define in what manner and with what people and on what sort of grounds and how long one ought to be angry; and in fact we sometimes praise men who err on the side of defect in this matter and call them gentle, sometimes those who are quick to anger and style them manly. However, we do not blame one who diverges a little from the right course, whether on the side of the too much or of the too little, but one who diverges more widely, for his error is noticed. For in fact no object of perception is easy to define; and such questions of degree depend on particular circumstances, and the decision lies with perception."[10]

The extremes of sinfulness and sainthood, associated with Christian dogma, were concepts foreign to the Greek mind. Nor could such qualities have suited a tragic hero. According to Aristotle, fear, an emotion essential to tragedy, arises from witnessing the suffering of a man like ourselves. To arouse the emotion of fear, necessary to tragic pleasure, the hero must be a man with whom the spectator can identify himself, a man predominantly good but not perfect. No one can identify himself with either saint or sinner.

And yet Aristotle, author of the doctrine of the mean, insists, "Not every action or emotion however admits of the observance of a due mean. Indeed the very names of some directly imply evil, for instance, malice, shamelessness, envy, and, of actions, adultery, theft, murder. All these and similar actions and feelings are blamed as being bad in themselves; it is not the excess or deficiency of them that we blame.[11]

Like Aristotle, the Greek tragedians and Shakespeare generally conceive of a universe in which some standards of morality are absolute[12] (albeit a universe in which the principle of *hamartia*, or missing the mark, has ample room to operate). In their works which may most properly be called tragedies there is little ambiguity either in their thinking or in their terminology. They call evil *evil*, and good *good*. And that there may be no mistaking the author's intent, a chorus sometimes, or sometimes a single character, whether protagonist or minor character, acts as a "Greek chorus" and asserts the ethical import.

Thus, evil is frankly acknowledged by Aeschylus' Clytemnestra and also by Shakespeare's Iago. Good is as clearly recognized by good characters, who speak of themselves as good: Brutus defending himself in the forum, Othello explaining his action in the senate, Hippolytus asserting his innocence before his father, Oedipus declaring his nobility to Teiresias, and Lear crying out in anguish:[13]

> *I am a man*
> *More sinn'd against than sinning.*

And that there may be no uncertainty about the moral basis of action, disinterested actors throughout the tragedy frequently give ethical commentary.

Moreover, at the conclusion of the tragedy, the nobility of the hero is often asserted. Thus, Edgar pays tribute to Lear and Horatio to the dying Hamlet, Antony speaks for Brutus, Cassio for Othello, Artemis for Hippolytus, and the chorus for Oedipus at Colonus. Likewise, the evil characters at the end of *Macbeth* are denounced by Malcolm as "this dead butcher and his fiend-like queen." The predominantly good man is declared innocent and the predominantly evil man guilty. The most notable Greek and Shakespearean tragedies base their action upon accountability, an idea reflected in the ancient law court, according to which man was declared either innocent or guilty with regard to his moral acts, and in accordance with which legal justice was administered.[14] A man cannot be both good and evil; the protagonist cannot be both hero and villain at the same time in the tragedy.

The Greeks, Seneca, and Shakespeare recognized tragedy

as inhering in the nature of life and frequently depicted it as an exaltation of human suffering. Further to understand the import of *ethos* it will be necessary to trace the course of action as it appears in analogous aspects in various tragedies.

TWO

POETIC JUSTICE

ARISTOTLE'S remarks on tragedy apply but little to Aeschylus. In the *Poetics* Aristotle ranks as distinctly inferior, tragedy ending with "an opposite catastrophe for the good and for the bad,"[1] that is, tragedy in which poetic justice is done, as in the freeing of the innocent Orestes and the condemnation of the guilty Macbeth.

Both tragedies end in the dispensation of a justice which is divinely sanctioned. It seems that because Aristotle had no theory of a moral relationship between god and man, no assumption that a just god governs man's actions on earth, such as is implicit in Aeschylean ethics and in the Christian doctrine of retribution, he did not give first rating to a tragedy which emphasizes the imposition of divine rewards and punishments.[2]

Macbeth has been compared to Clytemnestra as a study in degeneration of character through evil. However, Greek tragedy did not emphasize the progressive development of character in either the direction of increased or of decreased nobility. Clytemnestra, unlike Macbeth, is not shown at the beginning of the trilogy as a person of predominantly noble character. The Clytemnestra who dominates the action of *Agamemnon* is, to be sure, endowed with a modicum of good in spite of a preponderance of evil in her nature; but, although the murder of her husband to satisfy her duty of revenge has a slight justification, the chorus reminds her

8

that she is largely responsible and the *alastor* of the house of Atreus can be only the abettor in her guilt.

Aristotle held that it is the function of comedy to deal with "bad" men, because pity, he contends, is aroused by witnessing the spectacle of a man who suffers beyond his deserts, and merited suffering arouses little sympathy. "The pleasure, however, thence derived is not the true tragic pleasure. It is proper rather to Comedy," Aristotle argues.[3] Nicoll affirms, "Aristotle evidently believed the risible to lie in degradation; men, he says, are in comedy made worse than they are and consequently become objects of merriment."[4] However, the element of goodness apparent in the characters of both Macbeth and Clytemnestra raises them above the level of comic characters.

Both *Macbeth* and the *Oresteia* contain some excellent ironic episodes, but the resolution of neither is ironic. Thompson aptly points out, in referring to Aeschylus: "He was essentially a believer, not a doubter. He was, to be sure, troubled by ethical difficulties; it would be strange if any thoughtful man were not; and he dramatized one in the *Oresteia* and another in the *Prometheia*. But he resolved these problems, as a genuine ironist does not. *The Eumenides* tells us in effect that private vengeance must give way to civic justice; and the lost plays of the other trilogy undoubtedly reconciled the wisdom of Prometheus with the power of Zeus."[5] When rewards and punishments are issued according to deserts, we are in the realm of poetic justice.

9

The Oresteia and Macbeth

The Oresteia

ETHICAL elevation of tone is perhaps the salient feature of ancient Greek drama. Ethical import combined with tragic technique gave excellence to the work of Aeschylus, Sophocles, and Euripides, and became the distinguishing mark of the work of that other great tragic artist, Shakespeare; for ethical significance in drama implies that there are certain concepts of morality shared by intelligent men, and that all good art is grounded in a common moral territory, however much the philosophic and religious thinking of individual artists may vary.

Aeschylus built on that common moral territory deliberately, and it is he who first associated the name of tragedy with the idea of ethical grandeur, for to the Greek mind the good and the beautiful, the ethical and the esthetic, were inseparable in a work of art. Moreover, by consciously constructing a philosophic and religious background for his major work, the Oresteian trilogy, Aeschylus gave solidity to his massive structure.

It is a commonplace that Aeschylus transformed the traditional ideas about the gods by refining the older mythological conceptions. A transformation into the moral had been going on from the beginning in the mind of the religious Greek, but the tendency came to a rational expression in Aeschylus' representation of Zeus and lesser divinities as ultimate moral ideals in the Oresteia. In his justification of the ways of god to man in this trilogy, Aeschylus shows the evolution of supernatural powers which, after relinquishing certain naturalistic characteristics, survive with a growing moral significance.

The Greek people had long been familiar with the poets' stories of the gods, and since custom restricted Greek tragedy almost entirely to mythological or legendary subjects, it became inevitable that there should be constant repetition in the stories dramatized by the tragedians. Yet for the audience a repeated myth need not lose its freshness, for the restriction upon subject matter of the Greek theater did not prevent the dramatists' adapting the primitive tales to their own purpose. Thus the story of Agamemnon, which had been for Homer in the *Odyssey* a tale of treachery, murder, and revenge—treachery on the part of Aegisthus and Agamemnon's wife Clytemnestra, murder of Agamemnon at the hands of Aegisthus assisted by Clytemnestra, and justifiable revenge by Agamemnon's son Orestes—became for Aeschylus a solemn tracing of individual responsibility against a background of hereditary guilt. In the trilogy it is significant also that Aeschylus, unlike Homer, made Clytemnestra instigator of the crime, not Aegisthus.[6]

In the ancient legend of the house of Atreus, Aeschylus tries to find an explanation of man's suffering and to reach a clearer understanding of the nature of god. Increased motivation of character is Aeschylus' contribution to the primitive legend. Nevertheless, even for Aeschylus, motive is important only in so far as it is dramatically necessary to explain an act and to indicate that the act could have been avoided.

Aeschylus shows, for the most part, the continuity of guilt, crime engendering crime through the generations, for, "It is the deed of iniquity that begetteth more iniquity and like unto its own breed," says the chorus in *Agamemnon*, voicing the sentiment of Aeschylus. Because the race has a moral responsibility for the past, Aeschylus recognizes

11

that the family or the race which preserves certain dominant characteristics that are evil needs a corrective discipline of suffering to extirpate those evil tendencies. Aeschylus, therefore, insists that a tendency toward guilt is inherited. But the hereditary curse, conceived of in earlier times as the result of an immoral vindictiveness on the part of divine powers, appears in Aeschylus as an inherited though not insuperable tendency toward guilt, which the individual, by an act of will, may foster or resist. The chain of crime may at any link be broken.[7] Aeschylus does not allow men's free will to be annihilated, even in members of a tainted race.

The theme of retribution as a consequence of guilt is exemplified in characters who are in a limited sense free to choose their course.[8] Aeschylus does not ask, like Sophocles, what kind of characters would be likely to act in this manner, but what motives could have influenced otherwise noble characters to err thus. For Aeschylus the motive is frequently *hybris*, commonly translated *pride*.

Hybris—excessive pride in one's prosperity—which incurs the nemesis of the gods, is a familiar theme in Greek literature. Nemesis is the penalty of wrongdoing, especially of *hybris*, which has its roots in want of reverence for eternal ordinances and want of respect for the rights of human beings. Nemesis overtakes men most often in the hour of triumph, not because the gods are jealous but because men are then likely to be most reckless.[9]

Agamemnon's first act of *hybris*, the sacrifice of his daughter Iphigenia, was done not as an act of moral blindness, for Agamemnon had been forewarned by Calchas the seer that the consequences of his act would bring upon him "wrath that exacteth vengeance for a child." This wrath, the reporting chorus implies, will mean retaliation at the hands of Clytemnestra. Yet Agamemnon is justified as the agent of Zeus the Avenger in pursuing the war which Helen has instigated by her elopement with Paris. And Agamemnon is assured by Calchas that the heroism of his act of *hybris* will eventually bring success against Troy.

Agamemnon must decide between duty to his child and loyalty to the cause of his brother Menelaus and his allies in arms. He vacillates. The conflict of duties assumes a tragic import. Agamemnon is loath to sacrifice Iphigenia in order that the fleet may sail, even though he is obliged to appease Artemis for his unintentional slaughter of her sacred doe; yet, at the same time, he is under solemn obligation to Menelaus and to Zeus the Avenger to punish the *hybris* of Paris and the city which received him when he returned with Helen. Loyalty to one obligation involves disloyalty to another. The divine law bids and forbids at the same time. "Which of these courses is not fraught with ill?" he cries. Then, prompted by ambition, Agamemnon chooses disastrously in so far as later action in the drama is concerned—although we are not told what he might have suffered at the hands of Zeus had he failed, by refusing to appease Artemis with the sacrifice of Iphigenia, to transport his comrades to the siege of Troy.

Although the sacrifice of Iphigenia, narrated by the chorus in the first ode, occurred ten years before the tragedy opens, it is dramatically an event which takes place within the trilogy, for the past is a controlling element in the Aeschylean conception of tragedy. It is the function of the chorus, by such linkage, to affirm the moral vindication of events.

Because Agamemnon heeds only the proclamation of

Calchas, which will allow the ships to sail, and disregards the dire consequences, the hereditary curse of the house of Atreus, which was awaiting only an opening through some evil deed to exact its toll of blood, seizes upon him. But the curse does not operate immediately after the sacrifice of Iphigenia. Before the fulfillment of the curse (invoked by Thyestes, who long ago had been tricked by his brother Atreus, father of Agamemnon, into feasting on his own children) Agamemnon continues to triumph for ten years at Troy. But the earlier error induces another, and as a result of his propensity to err Agamemnon's guilt is ominously aggravated. For the death of countless Greek warriors at Troy, for the sacrilegious despoiling of the temples of the gods, and finally for his presumption in bringing home the captive Cassandra, Agamemnon will be punished. Cassandra, who had accepted Apollo's gifts but had refused to pay his price, who had retained her virginity by keeping a god at bay, has now been given to the king of men, and he in his continued acts of *hybris* presents his captive mistress as an affront to his wife. The purple carpet upon which Agamemnon treads at the instigation of Clytemnestra is the dramatic symbol of his cumulative acts of *hybris.*

Aeschylus implies that for the proud man the only discipline is adversity. The choral precept, "Wisdom cometh by suffering," attributed in *Agamemnon* to Zeus, affords firm ground for human action, even though Aeschylus does not develop this thought on the human level in the trilogy. His emphasis is rather on the evolving moral nature of the gods, under whose power the freedom of choice of the individual is limited.

But to ask whether Aeschylus believed in fate or in

14

freedom of the will is to ask an idle question. Like most men, he believed in both. Aeschylus' trilogy is a recognition of the fact that the world is not ruled by blind chance, since in the background of man's activity there appear certain insuperable powers against which man's freedom operates. But the problem of freedom of the will did not occur to Aeschylus in the form in which it confronts us. While leaving his characters their freedom, Aeschylus leads them into situations in which its exercise is inevitably disastrous. He confronts them again and again with dilemmas appearing as conflicting duties in which a choice is morally imperative but none is morally feasible.[10]

Why does Agamemnon suffer for the folly of his ancestors? Aeschylus neither ignores nor answers the question. Agamemnon is a member of a family haunted by a primal curse. But at the moment of crisis he must make a choice, and he elects a course fraught with disaster, though presumably his lot would have been equally disastrous had he chosen the alternative course. However, Zeus the Avenger, of the early part of the trilogy, by permitting Agamemnon to be faced with odds so desperate, reveals himself as not yet the just god of the final play. Zeus, too, will learn in time to distribute good and evil less capriciously.

Agamemnon, then, is a tragic hero, the victim largely of circumstances, though partly of his own character. The austere Aeschylean characterization presupposes that action proceeds from causes largely external, beyond the control of the tragic hero, and to a greater or less extent we admit this fact with regard to our own lives, even though we act as though we were free.[11]

But Clytemnestra is the dominant figure in *Agamemnon*, and it is with reference to her character that the plot of the drama moves. Clytemnestra is a conspirator who does not speak her mind until after the fulfillment of her purpose, and then only equivocally.

Agamemnon opens ominously. The lonely and weary watchman has been singing to keep himself awake, but his song turns into a lament for the house of Atreus: "...yet the house itself, could it but speak, might tell a tale full plain." The watchman starts a rhythm of apprehension which increases in intensity through the tragedy —the first joyful, then dejected, utterances of the herald, the hypocritical greeting of Clytemnestra to her husband, and finally the inspired ejaculations of Cassandra foretelling the commission of the murder.[12]

Clytemnestra, who has been described by the watchman as "woman in sanguine heart and man in strength of purpose," enters during the first choral ode and proceeds to light the sacrificial fires. The chorus addresses her, but she does not speak. Silently she goes about her work and silently departs. But even though she does not speak, Clytemnestra's purpose is revealed through the words of the chorus, which adumbrate what is passing in her mind. When she re-enters and speaks, the audience is ready to catch the hidden meaning of her words, which are the more impressive because so long delayed.

The queen proclaims the victory at Troy to an incredulous chorus, which she rebukes for questioning her announcement, for attributing it to belief in an idle dream. The audience knows she is dreaming of another victory. Then in a speech of heavy tone she utters the ironic prayer that Agamemnon, kept free from guilt towards the gods at Troy, may reach home safely and that "the grievous suffering of the dead" may not prove wakeful. She uses in referring to "the dead" the ambiguous plural so that the chorus will interpret it to mean the slaughtered Trojans —but the audience will know that it indicates her murdered daughter. She closes her invocation with a reference to her consummate conspiracy: "For, choosing thus, I have chosen the enjoyment of many a blessing." Clytemnestra's plan to welcome her husband is complete.

Clytemnestra's prayer as she leaves is followed closely by the message of the herald addressing the chorus of counsellors, commenting upon the *hybris* of Agamemnon and his men at Troy: "Demolished are the altars and the shrines of her gods; and the seed of her whole land hath been wasted utterly." When Agamemnon enters, the chorus, in its welcome to the king, reveals its apprehension as clearly as it may: "In course of time thou shalt learn by enquiry who of thy people have been honest, who unfitting, guardians of the State." But Agamemnon does not guess the truth. He promises to eliminate challengers in his kingdom—overlooking those in his household.

When Clytemnestra returns with her attendants, carrying purple tapestries, she is perturbed. She sees before her the man she has dreaded in her dream, and she knows that for one or the other the last hour has come. She attempts some statement of her case. By her effusive address she invites the nemesis of the gods, while seeming to deprecate it. Flattery of words leads to flattery of action, and she bids her attendants spread for Agamemnon the purple carpet, "that Justice may usher him to a home he ne'er hoped to see"—that nemesis may follow his overt act of *hybris* in accepting honor due only the gods.

Her proposal to tread the purple startles Agamemnon, but she appeals to his pride and he yields. To be honored almost as a god is the lot of the happiest kings. The temptation of happy Agamemnon is to consider himself more than mortal and to accept honors reserved only for the gods. Agamemnon compromises. With sandals removed as a sign of humility, and with a prayer that the nemesis of the gods may not strike him, he treads the purple carpet to the palace. But before he goes he affronts his wife with the command to care for his mistress Cassandra. Agamemnon enters the palace with words of trust, while Cassandra remains outside as emblem of his *hybris*. Meanwhile, Clytemnestra in her highly symbolic speech, "This is the sea (and who shall drain it dry?)," foreshadows the bloody murder she is about to commit.

Cassandra remains silent until Clytemnestra, impatient and angry, enters the palace. Cassandra's silence is effective. The audience knows she is seeing phantoms of another world. When Cassandra speaks, her gift of prophecy enables the audience to perceive the ethical unity of the story of the house of Atreus, involving the operation of the curse from the time of the banquet of Thyestes to the appearance of Orestes as avenger of Agamemnon and herself.

Cassandra's suffering has given her sympathy with suffering humanity. She is an example of noble endurance of the adversity that besets victor and vanquished alike. As a reminder of Agamemnon's *hybris*, Cassandra illustrates the fact that the wrong of an individual brings suffering not only to the wrongdoer but to innocent persons as well. Cassandra's prophetic utterances intensify the tragic moment by drawing the destiny of all mortals into harmony with her own. She is a symbol for the tragedy of the whole human race. Cassandra, at length, enters the palace, and captive and captor are confronted by the same death. The palace doors are opened and Clytemnestra stands revealed beside the bodies of her victims. The audience is now prepared for the revelation of the motives of the conspirators.

Clytemnestra admits her hypocrisy, which she defends as a means to an end which has now been accomplished. The horrified threats of the chorus she answers with denunciation of Agamemnon's sacrifice of his own child, and hers. She names Aegisthus as her protector, and in the same breath cries out against the faithlessness of her husband who lies at her feet with his concubine. She sees herself the incarnation of the curse of the house of Atreus, exacting its toll of blood from every generation. She will make a compact with the *alastor*, preferring to live in comparative poverty if the long series of mutual murders may be brought to an end.

It is impossible. Aegisthus appears, a coward and a bully, and a foil for the strong and wilful, resourceful and resolute Clytemnestra. Clytemnestra the chorus regards with awe in spite of its accusation, but in its attitude toward the bombastic Aegisthus there is but contempt. Although Aegisthus boasts, "I am he who planned this murder and with justice," attributing his main motive to a feud of his own with Agamemnon, Clytemnestra regards Aegisthus not as an accomplice in her crime but as her protector after the act.

Although the fate of Agamemnon at the hands of Zeus can in large degree be justified on account of the king's *hybris*, our sympathy is with the murdered king. The dignity of his position and the greatness of his achievements acclaimed by the sympathetic commentators are emphasized by the ignominy of his death. Here was a man, a king, slain by the hand of a woman. And if Agamemnon has been weighed in the scale of Justice and found wanting, Clytemnestra's hand is not less guilty on that account. Agamemnon hesitated before he slew Iphigenia, and he slew only upon divine command, but Clytemnestra killed calculatingly and in hate.

Clytemnestra hated Agamemnon for his unfaithfulness, yet she too was unfaithful. Agamemnon's concubine was Cassandra, the gift of a grateful army—a Trojan princess to be pitied for her staunch endurance of suffering. Clytemnestra's paramour is the contemptible adulterer Aegisthus, whom it is apparent she loves; but the queen's adultery, poetic justice as it were for Atreus' punishment of Thyestes' ancient adultery, is a criminal act which, introduced late in the drama, serves only to vitiate her plea for retributive justice.

Clytemnestra urges that the ancient curse pronounced by Thyestes upon the children of Atreus constrained her to become its incarnation, a claim which the chorus accepts only in part, since the ancestral *alastor* could at most be the abettor of her guilt, not the instigator. When the chorus calls upon her to seek purification, according to the ancient custom, if she slew her husband for Iphigenia's sake, she refuses.

The main motive that can be urged to extenuate the guilt of Clytemnestra is the moral obligation of a mother to avenge the murder of her child. Urging this, Clytemnestra assumes that she is guiltless and that her act has brought to an end the ancient curse of the house. The chorus denies her plea, although the old counsellors recognize that she is not altogether culpable.

Clytemnestra is the victim of the Aeschylean dilemma, which emphasizes the fact that a character can do what is right and morally enjoined from one point of view only by doing what is wrong and forbidden from another. Accordingly, the crime of Clytemnestra is not wholly villainous. Of the impulses of which it is the result, one at least is noble. But the agent fulfilling the curse is never wholly innocent. During the course of events Clytemnestra was free to choose her action, and her decision sprang not from a sense of duty alone but from a mixture of baser motives. If she thus, by a wrong choice, made herself the instrument of the curse, she also made herself its object.

When *The Libation-Bearers* opens, Clytemnestra, who in *Agamemnon* had refused to put credence in dreams and who had failed to expiate her villainy by lustral rites, has as a result of an ominous dream dispatched her daughter Electra and the chorus of slave women to offer propitiatory sacrifices at Agamemnon's tomb. Clytemnestra now puts faith in visions. She recognizes her guilt, on the night before her murder, and is terrified by a dream of a serpent that she has borne and suckled, and that bites her.

The chorus expresses doubt as to the efficacy of libations in washing away blood, and the offerings are thereafter turned to another purpose by Electra, the chorus, and the returning Orestes. With the offerings, the suppliants invoke the ghost of Agamemnon as aid in their vengeance. The ghost of Agamemnon, thus conjured up by affection, though unseen and unspeaking, makes palpable to the audience the moral claims of the dead king.

Orestes, who in *Agamemnon* had been sent away as a boy to an ally, Strophius in Phocis (presumably to serve Clytemnestra's purpose but ostensibly for his own safety), has now returned a young man and is ready to vindicate the claims of his murdered father. Although Orestes has some human motives for matricide—namely, his filial duty to avenge a father who has been dishonorably slain and ignobly buried, as well as his just ambition to recover his patrimony—it is necessary to the drama that his motives be obscured, for Orestes is acting at the command of Apollo, who will become his defendant in a larger issue in the final play of the trilogy.

The long *commos*, in which the chorus, Electra, and Orestes participate, creates an atmosphere of vengeance in which repetition of the idea of blood for blood palliates the matricide of Orestes. It is necessary that Orestes steel himself for the murder of his mother in cold blood, and the dirge serves that purpose.

The shifting interplay of intensified moods in the *commos* is like a piece of counterpoint in which two varying themes are played in long crescendo—the lament for the murdered king against the prayer for vengeance.[13] At the beginning of the chant Orestes and Electra are lamenting their father's death while the chorus is urging them to pray for vengeance; at the end of the dirge the chorus is lamenting and brother and sister are crying out for revenge. It is significant, however, that the chorus is now advancing the movement of the drama by lamenting not the past of the house of Atreus but the ominous future.

Orestes and Electra have been strengthened in their resolve, so that when the chant ceases they continue to cry out for vengeance, and the invocation at the tomb ends in a magnificent coda which serves to determine Orestes in his execution of the double murder. Clytemnestra's dream of the serpent—a serpent which Orestes identifies with himself—becomes his final incentive.

Since Orestes has earlier received from Apollo a command to avenge his father's death by killing his mother, the counterpoise of moral obligations in the trilogy is now absolute. To disobey Apollo would result in punishment of Orestes by the Erinyes of his father, avengers of a murdered parent. To follow Apollo's injunction will result in pursuit of Orestes by the Erinyes of his mother. Orestes realizes he is in an impasse in which action is humanly indefensible. Yet act he must, for to fail to act would be to leave his father unavenged. A choice is morally imperative, but none is morally feasible. However, unlike his father Agamemnon, Orestes faces the dilemma with defensible motives, backed by the promise of Apollo to exculpate him after the deed.

Orestes appears in disguise at his mother's palace and announces himself dead. Clytemnestra, feigning sorrow, conceals her joy, but Orestes' babbling affectionate nurse, lamenting her darling's death, reports her mistress' hypocrisy: "Before the servants, indeed, behind eyes that made sham gloom she hid her laughter over what hath befallen happily for her."

The nurse's homely reminiscences, her rambling account of her troubles incidental to nursing, arouse sympathy for Orestes who, like other mortals, was once a helpless infant laid at a woman's breast. Also, the contrast between the unnatural mother and the devoted slave serves to lessen the sympathy for Clytemnestra later when, with breast bared before her son's sword, she pleads her motherhood and her wrongs; when she cries, "Have pity, child, upon this breast at which full oft, sleeping the while, with toothless gums thou didst suck the milk that nourished thee. . . ." Orestes is constrained to hesitate until Pylades reminds him of Apollo's oracle.

Clytemnestra, hearing the cryptic report of Aegisthus' death—"The dead are killing the living"—grasps the irony of the situation immediately, and displaying her old resourcefulness she cries, "By guile we are to perish even as we slew. Someone give me a battle-axe, and quick!" Although she recognizes the fulfillment of her dream, she meets the danger with her old defiance.

She attempts to save herself by pleading with her son. She implores pity she has not shown to others. She presents specious excuses in extenuation of her guilt: fate, woman's frailty, and Agamemnon's infidelity. It is significant that Iphigenia has now been forgotten. Orestes' deed seems therefore less abhorrent.

After the double murder Orestes invokes sympathy by displaying the robe in which his father was murdered, stained with his father's blood. But as he stands triumphantly over the bodies of Clytemnestra and Aegisthus, on the stage where once lay Agamemnon and Cassandra, as he spreads out before him the emblem of his victims' guilt in justification of his deed, he realizes that his "victory is a pollution unenviable," and madness comes upon him. The Erinyes of his mother are at work, and he goes, an exile, to seek purification at the shrine of Apollo in Delphi.

As *The Eumenides* opens the innocent Orestes is still the object of the curse even though it does not perpetuate itself through his act or destroy him as a victim. Ancient justice required that the shedding of blood be punished irrespective of motive, and it is the obligation of the Erinyes to enforce this ancient justice.

The Erinyes represent one aspect of the moral order, that of primitive society in which tribal custom exacts an eye for an eye, a life for a life. The Erinyes are inexorable and absolute. They know no justification for crime; they are interested only in avenging the deed for which primitive law provides no redress.[14] But the Apolline ritual of purification symbolizes an attempt of the state to take into account motives for action, and because Orestes is innocent Apollo purifies him of blood guilt.[15] Thus Aeschylus illustrates in his trilogy the manner in which moral and religious ideas develop in response to changes in the structure of society.[16]

The Erinyes, however, do not recognize the sanction of the Delphic god to release Orestes from moral responsibility. They do not admit introduction of the ritual to terminate the ancient feud. The conflict then centers in a dispute between certain moral powers of the universe, with Orestes the bone of contention.

The persecuted Orestes, having received from Apollo ceremonial purification of the physical stain of blood, now arrives at Athens where he seeks absolution from the moral stain of guilt, in order that he may return to Argos. Orestes faces trial at Athens in the newly established court of the Areopagus. To Athens the Erinyes have pursued Orestes, like a pack of hounds on the scent.

The contending parties are Apollo and the Erinyes. Apollo claims that his testimony is incontrovertible because it comes from Zeus, a claim confirmed by Athena; the Erinyes appeal to the Fates, whose decrees they have been appointed to safeguard. Behind the dispute, then, of Apollo and the Erinyes there lies a deeper discord, for Zeus and the Fates are at variance.

At the trial of Orestes for homicide the prosecuting Erinyes speak first. They ask Orestes whether he did the deed of which he is accused, how, and why. Their questioning indicates that the court will consider not only the act but also the motives for the action. It indicates that the *ius naturale* is about to yield to the *ius civile*, and that absolute standards of primitive society are about to be superseded by recourse to reason embodied in equity.[17]

As the case stands, both the murder of Agamemnon and the murder of Clytemnestra have some moral justification, but each murder is also a crime. The two wrongs, representing different levels of social morality, therefore constitute for Orestes a dilemma which in terms of human justice is insoluble. The tie vote of the jurors recognizes the moral claims of both Apollo and the Erinyes, each representing a partial conception of justice. The issue is finally decided by Athena, who as spokesman of a new Zeus with whom Fate is now reconciled, interprets not law but divine sanctions. Orestes is exonerated. Orestes is delivered from a rigid fate by a change in the attitude of the Erinyes who, after the intervention of Athena, become the gracious but still-to-be-feared Eumenides.

The acquittal of Orestes marks the reign of a new social order, in which purely private vengeance is abolished and the state takes over the right to pass judgment in cases of homicide, and thus itself becomes the avenger of slain men. In the aetiological symbol of the Areopagus, the first court in Athens to try a case of homicide, Aeschylus has expressed his ideal of a moral governance of the world, which demands that not only the deed but also the intention of the doer be taken into consideration, that a distinction be made between voluntary and involuntary error, and that only wilful error knows no acquittal. From the standpoint of Orestes in the Aeschylean trilogy, innocence is rewarded and poetic justice is meted out in the end.

Macbeth

As ORESTES' innocence is rewarded by acquittal, so Macbeth's guilt is punished by death, and an "opposite catastrophe" closes each play. Poetic justice is done in the end.

Although "brave Macbeth" is depicted as a good man at the beginning of the tragedy, his character gradually degenerates until at the end he is no longer a worthy thane but "this dead butcher." Aroused early by the thought of kingship promised by the witches, who "have more in them than mortal knowledge," and goaded by the affectionate ambition of his wife, whose desire to see her husband crowned will not permit her to contemplate the consequences of crime, Macbeth, who before the murder of Duncan could declare to his wife, "I dare do all that may become a man," is by persuasion about to satisfy his ambition and become, as Lady Macbeth promises, "so much more the man." "Disdaining Fortune," even as in battle, Macbeth embarks upon a series of crimes with complete knowledge of his infraction of moral law.

At this point it may be argued in extenuation of Macbeth's guilt that his evil acts are done under suasion, and by reason of what Aristotle would call "weakness of will."[18] He wants the crown, but he wishes to gain it innocently. Yet it is evident at the beginning, when the witches approach Macbeth on the heath, that his thoughts have not been wholly innocent. It is evident that he has previously entertained ambitious desires when, unlike his companion Banquo, he presses for further revelation.

The first prophecy of the witches, that Glamis shall be thane of Cawdor, is fulfilled. Macbeth is encouraged. But the king yet lives. Macbeth reflects:

> If it were done when 'tis done, then 'twere well
> It were done quickly. If the assassination

Could trammel up the consequence, and catch
With his surcease success; that but this blow
Might be the be-all and the end-all here....

Then he remembers that judgment is passed upon the assassin and justice done on this earth, even though it be possible to "jump the life to come."

Urged by his wife to murder Duncan, who has come to his castle "in double trust," as guest and as sovereign, Macbeth vacillates. Like Aeschylus' Clytemnestra, who spreads the purple carpet, Lady Macbeth appeals to her husband's pride in his former valor. It is significant that the deterrents to crime, not the incentives, are foremost in his mind. He recognizes that he is about to do evil but, fortified by wine, he yields. It is noteworthy too that, having murdered Duncan, Macbeth cannot complete his task. He must leave to his wife the act of smearing the grooms with the incriminating blood.

Macbeth makes his choice according to the principle of freedom of the will enunciated by both Aristotelian and Christian ethics. Aristotle holds that the choice between good and evil is equally voluntary, for the ability to act implies the ability not to act. Nor does the plea that no other action is possible at the time for a person of such a character excuse the perpetrator of evil. Aristotle considers that character is the result of habits which in turn were produced by a previous series of free choices.[19] Likewise, Christian ethics, upon which the tragedy of Macbeth at war with his conscience is based, holds that man was created by God to sin or not to sin, and if he chooses evil he "falls" through his own choice.

The initial crime, the murder of Duncan, Macbeth does in horror. Before the crime he envisages the bloody dagger, and after the crime "amen" sticks in his throat, and he cannot sleep. In an agony of remorse he cries, "Wake Duncan with thy knocking! I would thou couldst!" In the process of gaining the crown he has cast away his "eternal jewel." Macbeth's warring conscience, no longer that of a good man, impels him to evil, and he suborns the murder of Banquo. With heart now hardened against crime, he can affirm, "I have almost forgot the taste of fears."

As in the appearance of the "air-drawn dagger" and the voice that cried, "Sleep no more!" Macbeth's tortured imagination is active. He perceives the ghost of Banquo, murdered father of a line of kings, sitting in the royal seat Banquo's heirs will occupy. Conscience, a Christian nemesis, is oppressing Macbeth. Nemesis pursues Macbeth as it pursued Clytemnestra. But it is significant that, although Macbeth feels remorse keenly, his conscience never drives him to a course of action which might be called repentance.[20] By a series of evil acts, Macbeth is resolved to put his mind at rest; through fear he is led to perpetrate crime lest crime recoil upon him.

After the destruction of Banquo, in an increased effort to harden his conscience, Macbeth wades more deeply into blood with the command to destroy Macduff's household. His conscience has now become so callous that he can affirm, "I have almost forgot the taste of fears."

At length Macbeth no longer needs Lady Macbeth to impel him to evil. The futility of her self-abnegating effort to promote her husband's position is apparent shortly before the murder of Banquo when she realizes

Nought's had, all's spent,
Where our desire is got without content.

Nevertheless, in the banquet scene she attempts still to

cover her husband's guilt, as she did after his first crime when she smeared the sleeping grooms with Duncan's blood. But she is weary of her work. In answer to Macbeth's resolution to continue his criminal course, when he declares,

> *I am in blood*
> *Stepp'd in so far that, should I wade no more,*
> *Returning were as tedious as go o'er,*

Lady Macbeth's pathetic comment is only, "You lack the season of all natures, sleep." Thereafter her sleeplessness will lead to her sleep-walking insanity.

Before the execution of the deed her thoughts were occupied with ambitious plans to wade through blood in order to advance her husband; she lacked Macbeth's imagination to picture the consequences. Now her conscience cannot bear the load of accumulated guilt. She cannot wash away the memory of the regicide, the murder of Banquo, and the slaughter of Lady Macduff, and she dies in despair, possibly by her own hand. The death of Lady Macbeth evokes the pathos of insanity, which exonerates her partially from responsibility.

For Macbeth, the recollection of the man he was—the brave and honorable thane of Glamis—before, as treasonable thane of Cawdor, he murdered Duncan, emphasizes the futility of his ill-gotten kingship. When Macbeth affirms,

> *I have liv'd long enough. My way of life*
> *Is fallen into the sear, the yellow leaf;*
> *And that which should accompany old age,*
> *As honour, love, obedience, troops of friends,*
> *I must not look to have,*

he realizes that he has gained as a result of his effort only a "barren sceptre."

Nevertheless, although Macbeth grasps the futility of his murders, he will not acknowledge defeat. Contemptuous of life—the "walking shadow"—he remains resolute in the face of death. At the end, deceived by the witches' prophecies, but like Clytemnestra calling for the battle-axe, he dies defiantly presenting his shield.

> *Lay on, Macduff,*
> *And damn'd be he that first cries, "Hold, enough!"*

In his death Scotland is freed of a usurper, and Macduff has gained personal revenge. Malcolm, the rightful heir, will be crowned at Scone.

The tragic sympathy felt for Macbeth arises from the spectacle of suffering endured by a man whose conscience is continually resisting evil, even though his hands are constantly committing crimes. At the beginning of the tragedy Macbeth is a heroic warrior; but he is ambitious, and he is tempted. Initially he is aware of the error of his choice when he yields to the murder of Duncan, for he foresees that

> *This even-handed justice*
> *Commends th' ingredients of our poison'd chalice*
> *To our own lips.*

Yet he persists in his crimes, and the "air-drawn dagger" which at first led him to Duncan ultimately leads him to his death. As Aeschylus' Agamemnon, whose initial act of *hybris* leads to others, Macbeth goes from one bloody deed to another of deeper hue. Macbeth is a tragic hero not because of but in spite of the ignominy which closes his career. As Aristotle discovered, the spectacle of any human suffering evokes a measure of pity, even though, as in the case of Macbeth, defeat seems well deserved and poetic justice is accorded in the end.

31

THREE

POETIC IRONY

ARISTOTLE most admired those Sophoclean tragedies based on a conception of *ethos* which, granting that a man may suffer undeservedly, yet conceives of an ultimate justice in which the merit of those who suffer vindicates the moral order. Sophoclean *ethos* is thus asserted not in terms of poetic justice as seen from the narrower viewpoint of the individual sufferer but in terms of a universal apprehension of justice.[1]

From the standpoint of the individual, suffering results from an irony inherent in the universe. Of the irony of Sophocles, Thompson says, "His irony, as we noted earlier, arose from his choice of tragic theme—the fall of a great character with a flaw;—a fall that inevitably entails a contradiction between good fortune and calamity. For this hero, we feel, as Aristotle said, pity and fear."[2] Using Oedipus as an example, Thompson shows that while it is the *hamartia*, or tragic flaw, which brings about the destruction of an admirable character, emphasis in the tragedy is rather on the nobility of the protagonist than on the tragic flaw. In fact, the *hamartia* is a defect of a noble quality, a deviation from Aristotle's middle-of-the-road doctrine. Referring to Oedipus, Thompson continues: "If he had not been impetuous and hot-tempered, he would never, for example, have attacked the old man at the crossroads, for he was well aware of the oracle that declared he should slay his own father. The defects of his qualities which in other circumstances make him a wise and benignant ruler lead him in the particular circumstances of the play to his undoing. That is the irony of his fate; but his fate comes of his own character. Sophocles took a fatalistic legend, but carefully developed it in an unfatalistic fashion."[3]

It should be noted that Thompson speaks of "circumstances," not "fate," as opposing Oedipus, and observes, "I say 'circumstances,' not Fate, because for more than a century altogether too much has been parroted about Sophoclean 'fatalism' by writers who have got their ideas from other critics rather than from a study of the plays themselves."[4]

The Greeks had no word for what has been called variously dramatic, tragic, or Sophoclean irony, and which I have here called "poetic" irony because the term seems more inclusive.[5] "You have been told," observes Sedgewick, "that the Greeks had no *word* to describe the effect or principle that we call dramatic irony. So far as I know, they never really mention the *thing*, though they must have been affected by it even more strongly than we are when we read their plays—comedies as well as tragedies, but particularly the latter."[6] And he finds that "irony is implicit in the principle of Reversal of Fortune which Aristotle notes as the basis of tragedy; its general and its specific form are both implicit in his doctrine of Recognition or Discovery."[7] Worcester finds that "irony in its own right has expanded from a minute verbal phenomenon to a philosophy, a way of facing the cosmos."[8] And Sedgewick perceives, " ... it *heightens* the sense of pity and terror."[9]

Irony operates through the element of *ethos*. A glance at the titles of plays included in this section on poetic irony will suggest something of the significance of this aspect of *ethos*.

Oedipus the King and *Othello*

Oedipus the King

AESCHYLUS and Sophocles, who was a younger contemporary of Aeschylus and for a decade a rival tragedian, exploited the religious and moral ideas found in the same store of ancestral legends. But Sophocles came to express more fully than Aeschylus the ethical thought of his age.

Both tragedians attain, in their most mature work, a conception of a moral order under the sovereign rule of Zeus. But they differ in their conception of the nature of the forces which might explain the tragic experience, and therefore in their interpretation of human suffering.

Aeschylus believed in a beneficent power which dispenses rewards and punishments ultimately on the basis of unerring justice. Characteristically in Sophoclean tragedy (according to Aristotle's analysis of *Oedipus the King*, an example of the "perfect tragedy") the supreme power asserts itself not in terms of rewards and punishments for the individual but in a more universal kind of justice which reveals that the good, considered as a group, are not utterly destroyed, nor are the bad, considered as a group, ultimately triumphant, even though Sophocles regularly allows that one of the protagonists shall fall. Yet, granted that the bad do not ultimately triumph, a particularly base man need not be destroyed—for destruction of a villain would not arouse pity and fear, pity arising from undeserved misfortune and fear from the suffering of a man like ourselves.

Thus Sophocles gains probability in tragedy—or the representation of life as it is.[10]

Punishment implies guilt, and the notion that an innocent man might be punished for the sins of his fathers seems to have been a moral contradiction repugnant to both Aeschylus and Sophocles, for responsibility for guilt is intransferable.[11] Primitive belief that divine vindictiveness imposes suffering upon a victim of another's guilt, is purified by the Greek tragedians, so that even a family curse is no longer conceived of as inherited. As Aeschylus' *Oresteia* reveals, the gods ultimately sanction a termination of the ancient blood-feud. "For the curse is now conceived by Aeschylus to be nothing absolute, but rather a terrible hereditary propensity that reappears in successive generations; but each individual is free to yield to it or to resist," Greene discovers.[12] However, both Aeschylus and Sophocles observe that the innocent man may and does suffer for the action of the guilty, a fact verified in the natural order.

Sophocles, unlike Aeschylus, emphasizes the fact that suffering and guilt are not necessarily related causally, that suffering is not always penal, and that the good do not always prosper nor the bad incur punishment. Sophocles was aware of aspects of suffering unperceived by Aeschylus. Undeserved suffering always appears in Sophocles as a part of the evil inherent in an otherwise orderly universe.[13] It is that residuum of evil which cannot be explained on moral grounds—a tragically ironic fact of life. Sophocles therefore does not, like Aeschylus, construct a theodicy in which fate punishes guilt. Fate for Sophocles is perceived in terms of ironic experience, as in *Oedipus the King*.

Unmerited suffering serves in Sophocles to deepen the meaning of the Aeschylean inheritance which affirmed that

35

"wisdom cometh by suffering." It serves to strengthen noble character; man learns that he has unsuspected powers of endurance. Indeed, the stronger the outward forces against which man contends, the more impressive is the assertion of the human will. The most perfect example of a man upon whom adversity has had an enlightening influence is Oedipus as he appears in the tragedy which represents Sophocles' most mature thought on the theme, *Oedipus at Colonus:*

> ... *For I am taught by suffering to endure,*
> *And the long years that have grown old with me,*
> *And last not least, by true nobility.*

Oedipus, a man endowed with a noble nature, has learned in the course of time to surmount adversity.

However, there is no suggestion in Sophocles that wisdom justifies the suffering, because Sophocles does not, as does Aeschylus, demand for his tragedy gods who are always just, although justice is the distinguishing characteristic of Zeus in *Oedipus at Colonus.* And because Sophocles does not see in suffering merely the working of retributive justice, he is able to accept the popular legends with but slight reinterpretation. Nevertheless, the primitive elements of legend which Sophocles retains, those elements which suggest popular superstition and which do not conform to the laws of higher morality, he usually places outside the action of the drama.[14]

Sophocles, reinterpreting the Theban legend in *Oedipus the King,* leaves outside the action of the tragedy the crime of Laius and the warning of Apollo. He thus eliminates divine improbability from his plot and bases the action solidly upon character. In Sophocles the extraneous improbabilities antecedent to the plot correspond to the world of circumstance, to the tragic facts of life which we admit but cannot explain. Apollo and his oracle may be viewed poetically as the world of circumstance which human nature opposes. Sophocles neither justifies Apollo by making Oedipus a criminal nor condemns Apollo because the suffering of Oedipus is undeserved. He asks his audience to face the facts.

Oedipus the King offers an excellent example of Sophocles' idea of *ethos*, for in his tragedies he was concerned chiefly with the suffering of noble character, not wholly blameless, confronting inexorable and sometimes unpredictable powers. Oedipus was at first a happy man. He is recognized by the priest of Zeus as "first of men," second to the gods alone, and he refers to himself as the "foremost Theban in all Thebes." Reasonable above the rest, he has solved the riddle of the Sphinx who oppressed the Thebans —the Sphinx embodying the idea of a physical and mental force with which mortals precariously cope. As the reader of the Sphinx's riddle, Oedipus has been awarded the throne of his father Laius by a grateful people. He has become successor not only to the throne of Laius but also to "his bed, his wife"—in total ignorance. In total ignorance he has slain his father at the place where three roads meet, married his mother Jocasta, and begotten by her four children.

Oedipus' motives are good. Yet as a result of his solicitude for the state, of his attempt to spare his people suffering from the plague, he at length discovers that he himself is the polluter, the cause of the plague. Because he is concerned also about his reputation and his safety, he realizes that action is necessary. Thus he affirms:

Not for some far-off kinsman, but myself,
Shall I expel this poison in the blood;
For whoso slew that king might have a mind
To strike me too with his assassin hand.

The noble Oedipus, honored by his subjects, loved by his family—guilty of patricide and incest—unconsciously proclaims himself an outlaw when he pronounces the curse on the unknown murderer whose pollution has brought the plague on the land, and adds:

...I
His blood-avenger will maintain his cause
As though he were my sire....

By acting in the interest of the state Oedipus has, ironically, acted counter to his own interests.

The story of *Oedipus the King* is concerned with the gradual discovery of the king as the incestuous patricide and the revelation of Oedipus as the agent of his own guilt. The resoluteness of Oedipus, who presses on step by step to the discovery of his past, makes the tragedy.

The impetuosity which characterized Oedipus antecedent to the drama is exactly that which he manifests in the tragedy and which brings about his downfall. If he had not had the resolution to probe to the bottom of questions, he would never have gone to Delphi to discover his parentage. If he had employed greater restraint, he would never have slain Laius at the crossroads. In fact, if Oedipus had been as reasonable as Creon there would have been no tragedy of Oedipus, for Creon lacks both the weakness and the strength which equally betray Oedipus.[15]

Oedipus is confident, impulsive, resourceful, and generally reverent toward the gods. But his tendency to unrestrained anger, his tendency to let passion outstrip his reason, are gradually revealed. Yet his hasty temper, though inducing his downfall, does not impugn the essential goodness of his character.

His dominant characteristic, an imperious will, Oedipus manifests in the scene with Teiresias, when he commands the blind prophet to interpret the oracle of Apollo and to declare the murderer of Laius. Teiresias is the mouthpiece of Apollo, and Apollo's oracle is the will of Zeus interpreted. Teiresias is reluctant to speak. He tries to withhold his disastrous knowledge from Oedipus. Oedipus insults him, and Teiresias answers:

> *Thou blam'st my mood and seest not thine own*
> *Wherewith thou art mated. . . .*

Then, accused by Oedipus of being an accomplice in the crime, Teiresias is forced to pronounce Oedipus the polluter. Oedipus' anger increases, anger breeds suspicion, and Oedipus suspects Creon of being an abettor in a design to depose him. He concludes that Teiresias has been bribed by the ambition of Creon. Finally, taunted because of his blindness, the old seer declares:

> *. . . thou hast eyes,*
> *Yet see'st not in what misery thou art fallen,*
> *Nor where thou dwellest nor with whom for mate.*

Before he goes, Teiresias foretells Oedipus' dire future. Teiresias represents the divine foresight of Apollo as opposed to the human blindness of Oedipus. Oedipus cannot believe that he who had the inordinate acumen to read the Sphinx's riddle has erred blindly. "Twit me with that wherein my greatness lies," he charges Teiresias, and Tei-

resias answers, "And yet this very greatness proved thy
bane." Had Oedipus been less acute in answering the
riddle and thus saving the state, he had never been
awarded the kingdom of Thebes, nor had he ever married
the queen, his mother.

Creon has heard of Oedipus' accusation against him. He
enters, injured dignity incarnate. Oedipus charges him immediately, "My murderer and the filcher of my crown," and
refuses to listen to Creon's shrewd admonition:

> If thou dost count a virtue stubbornness,
> Unschooled by reason, thou art much astray.

In a long passage of *stichomythia* Creon calmly answers
the questions of Oedipus, while Oedipus attempts in his
interrogation to fix the blame on Creon. Oedipus has lost
the ability to distinguish friend from foe: he finds the
charges against him inconceivable.

In a speech of loyal candor, in answer to the unjust
aspersions of Oedipus, Creon shows that he himself has
nothing to gain by disloyalty. At the climax of the alterca-
tion Oedipus, still assured of his own integrity, implies that
he is determined to retain his rule. Jocasta enters and inter-
cedes for her brother Creon, and after the intervention of
the chorus of judicious counsellors, Oedipus yields sullenly.
The violent scenes with Teiresias and with Creon have dis-
turbed the chorus. They chant their hope that Oedipus is
not guilty of such deeds of *hybris* as are characteristic of
the traditional tyrant.

When Oedipus informs Jocasta of Teiresias' oracular accusation, Jocasta, although she believes in the gods, dis-
closes her mistrust of their human mouthpieces. Prophets
may be wrong. She attempts to give her husband peace

of mind by discrediting the seer—but her words have the opposite effect and serve only to strengthen Oedipus' apprehension. His first clue which will lead to discovery of his guilt comes with Jocasta's mention that Laius was slain "at a spot where three roads meet." Further information from Jocasta leads Oedipus to suspect that he has slain Laius, though "one" robber with "many" cannot square[16]— and has he not been more than once assured that Laius was slain by "robbers"?

It is significant in the light of later developments that Jocasta, recalling her castaway son, cannot bring herself to reveal to Oedipus the entire truth of his exposure during infancy. It was Laius, she says, who gave the infant with ankles pierced to the herdsman to be cast away; but later Oedipus learns from the herdsman that it was Jocasta herself.

Oedipus' strong presentiment that he has slain Laius and thus brought the pollution on the land is revealed when he tells Jocasta the story of his life: the taunt at Corinth, the visit to Delphi, and the encounter at the triple crossroads in Phocis, where he was attacked and where he slew his aggressor. He does not yet know that Laius is his father, for did not Polybus and Merope, the king and queen of Corinth, assure him, against the taunts of the drunken roisterer, that he was their son? Oedipus, fearing that he has pronounced the curse of banishment on himself, cries in anguish:

> If one should say, this is the handiwork
> Of some inhuman power, who could blame
> His judgment?

One loophole of escape remains for Oedipus. If the herdsman insists that Laius was slain by "robbers," as he has previously averred, Oedipus is excused; but if he says "one lonely wayfarer," the initial link in the chain of guilt is forged. Jocasta suspects that Oedipus may be the murderer. She therefore tries to deter his further investigation. She tries to discourage his summoning the herdsman eye-witness, the sole survivor. But Oedipus is determined to find the truth. Jocasta sends for the herdsman.

While Oedipus and Jocasta await the herdsman's arrival, a Corinthian messenger enters. The Corinthian dispels Oedipus' fears momentarily with the news that Polybus, his putative father, is dead. In the first shock of grief, believing that he can no longer become the murderer of his father, Oedipus doubts the Pythian prophecy. But a recoil returns him to his old reverence for the god, and he remembers that there yet remains the possibility of marriage with his mother. Later the messenger, hoping to relieve Oedipus of this fear, informs him that he is not the son of Polybus and Merope. The ironic reversal of situation only Jocasta apprehends. "Yet if no child of his, he loved me well," Oedipus reflects. He has longed to discover his parentage not only through fear of fulfillment of the oracle but also through filial affection.[17] From this moment he forgets his former fears in the desire to find his parents.

When the messenger announces that it was he who received Oedipus as an infant from "one of Laius' house," Jocasta is confirmed in the realization against which she has been struggling. She implores Oedipus to cease his search. "Enough the anguish *I* endure," she pleads—which in the Greek may mean also, "I am enduring *enough*."[18] Oedipus takes the second meaning. He thinks Jocasta is afraid that he may be proved a man of servile birth. His pride is touched. But he presses for further proof—he is resolved to search to the end. With a cry of despair, Jocasta rushes out.

In a speech marking the climax of the confidence of Oedipus, he calls himself, "Fortune's favourite child," one exalted above the vicissitudes of life. Oedipus forgets that fortune sometimes changes and brings evil also. And the chorus in a *hyporcheme*, a lively dance-song, here ironic and climactic, echoes the mood of Oedipus, and, by relieving the tension momentarily, heightens the tragic emotion of the scene that follows. The chorus also develops ironically the motif of the "first of men," introduced earlier in the drama—the chorus which in earlier *stasima* had contrasted the limited wisdom and power of mortals with the wisdom and power of Zeus—and hails Oedipus now as the son of a god, just before the self-sought truth shatters his happi-ness. At the moment when Oedipus calls himself the child of Fortune and thinks himself more than human, he is in greatest danger. The contrast between the seeming prosperity of a man like Oedipus and his actual situation, the possibility that apparent good may be evil, the anticipation of a reversal of fortune through nemesis which follows *hybris*, were what thrilled the Athenian audience and aroused their pity and fear.[19]

Like Aeschylus' Agamemnon, who was struck down as a result of *hybris* at the moment of his greatest triumph, Oedipus, at the pinnacle of glory, is about to fall with an ironic blow to the very depths of misery. Oedipus has violated the unwritten immemorial law which demands recognition of man's unstable lot—which enforces realiza-tion that power, riches, and honor rest on an insecure basis, that is, on the uncertain favor of the gods, and the greater

43

the height attained, the greater may be the fall. A similarly anxious thought is echoed by the chorus at the end of the play: "Therefore wait to see life's ending ere thou count one mortal blest."

Oedipus feels he has cause to rejoice. He has heard the evidence of the Theban herdsman (reported to him by Jocasta) which leaves no doubt in his mind that he has slain Laius, who is presumably not his father, and the evidence of the Corinthian which reveals that he is not the son of Polybus and Merope, thus relieving him of the possible guilt of both patricide and incest. The exaltation of Oedipus, contrasting so strongly with the despair of Jocasta, precedes the scene of recognition in which the Theban is confronted with the Corinthian and it is apparent that the slayer of Laius is guilty also of patricide and incest.

Oedipus, who now stands revealed as the slayer of his father and the husband of his mother, feels himself polluted and the polluter of all who come in contact with him. He experiences shame and remorse. As Aeschylus' Orestes became a defilement to Argos after the murder of his mother, so Oedipus, charged now with murder and with incest, has become a defilement to Thebes.

It was possible for a Greek of Sophocles' time to believe that certain conduct made a man physically unfit for human society, and yet to absolve him of moral blame. According to primitive ethics, which regards only the external act without taking cognizance of the internal act of will, the case of Oedipus constitutes a ritual defilement. But a more advanced ethics, taking into account the intention of the doer, and distinguishing between deeds done with open eyes and deeds done in ignorance, would recognize Oedipus

44

as morally innocent. As Orestes was proved innocent in the trial at Athens, so Oedipus will later be absolved in *Oedipus at Colonus* and by Aristotle in the *Poetics*. Oedipus himself makes a distinction between involuntary and voluntary evil when, immediately after blinding himself in his agony, he declares:

> *Apollo, friends, Apollo, he it was*
> *That brought these ills to pass;*
> *But the right hand that dealt the blow*
> *Was mine, none other.*

Oedipus blinds himself not only in remorse but also in the hope of finding forgetfulness by shutting out the world, the sight of wife and children and everything in Thebes that might remind him of his disaster; nor could he, as he later realizes, have endured the sight of his father and mother in Hades. He feels in the first torrent of anguish that blindness is not enough; he wishes he could make himself deaf as well. He wishes he had perished in infancy on Mount Cithaeron.

"Why didst thou give it then to this old man?" he had asked the Theban herdsman when he discovered that he was the infant who had been spared. And the herdsman —"Through pity, master, for the babe." Ironically Oedipus has been spared for a worse fate. But since he can no longer act but only suffer, the surge of his passion subsides and he affirms:

> *I myself must bear*
> *The load of guilt that none but I can share.*

Oedipus realizes now that death is no remedy for the "sin no gallows could atone." But how, living in the hope of expiating his crime, can he find life tolerable? As he reflects, he begins to discover a further significance in living, when he says to Creon:

> *For I had ne'er been snatched from death, unless*
> *I was predestined for some awful doom.*

The change of tone in this last scene prepares us for what Sophocles, at nearly ninety, will make of the cruel old legend of Oedipus, in *Oedipus at Colonus.*

As *Oedipus the King* closes, Oedipus' anxious thoughts turn with affectionate generosity to his daughters, whom he must leave a legacy of shame. For Antigone and Ismene, heirs of his misfortune, he asks:

> *Pray ye may find some home and live content,*
> *And may your lot prove happier than your sire's.*

Creon, who betrays no trace of malice after his harsh treatment by Oedipus earlier in the play, takes up the theme of *sophrosyne*, which requires that a man bear with restraint not only his good fortune but also those ills which are inevitable.

> *Crave not mastery in all,*
> *For the mastery that raised thee was thy bane*
> *and wrought thy fall.*

Sophocles has treated the tragedy of Oedipus as a conjunction of character and malignant circumstances, as a contrast between what Oedipus is and what he does in ignorance. The tragedy of *Oedipus the King* lies in the fact that here is a great man ironically ruined.

Othello

IN *Oedipus the King* the tragedy lies in the contrast between the noble intentions of the hero and his ignoble acts done in ignorance. In *Othello* there is a similar irony between what Othello is and what he does in ignorance.[20] Like Oedipus, Othello acts blindly because he is not able to penetrate the wiles of the villain, who is the Shakespearean counterpart of the inscrutable fate of Oedipus.

In each case an uncontrolled passion induces the hero's downfall. Although Oedipus has fulfilled the prophecy of the oracle previous to the opening of the play, the tragic weakness which he manifests during the action, in his effort to discover the cause of the plague, is exactly the kind of unreasoned action which led to the patricide. His wrathful temper is an obstacle to his understanding. Likewise, Othello's passion will dethrone reason and ultimately lead to the blind rage which impels him to murder his wife. Nevertheless (as is true in the case of Oedipus also), although Othello's reason is deluded by passion, that passion, while inducing his downfall, does not impugn the nobility of his character.

There is, however, this difference: Oedipus' fault arises primarily from devotion to state-interest; Othello's from self-esteem.[21] The wrath of Oedipus is also a measure of his innocence, for Oedipus is assured of his integrity and is determined to retain his good name, which is linked with the welfare of the state. After the first act, Othello's energy, which previously had been directed entirely to the military service of the state, is gradually diverted by sexual jealousy until, in an effort to save his personal honor, he is driven to relinquish his occupation and bid:

> *Farewell the tranquil mind! farewell content!*
> *Farewell the plumed troops and the big wars*
> *That make ambition virtue!*

47

Othello's tragedy, like the tragedy of Oedipus, lies in the fact that here is a man whom "passion could not shake" overcome by a force powerful enough and malignant enough to excite that passion to a destructive end. Iago is the embodiment of that fatal force. Ostensibly Iago's villainy is motivated. He hates the Moor. He bears a grudge against Othello because the general has promoted Cassio to the lieutenancy of which the ensign Iago considers himself more deserving. Another pretext Iago offers for hatred of the Moor is sexual jealousy, for Iago suspects both Othello and Cassio of intimacy with his wife Emilia. For his consummate villainy Iago can give no reason wholly adequate. Nevertheless, he is determined, as he says, to

> *Make the Moor thank me, love me, and reward me*
> *For making him egregiously an ass*
> *And practising upon his peace and quiet*
> *Even to madness.*

At the outset Iago has no preconceived plan; his wish is only to avenge himself by humiliating Othello and to regain his self-esteem by getting Cassio's place. He shapes his intrigue gradually and as opportunity affords. The machinations of the villain are slowly revealed as Iago grapples Othello in his toils by insinuation and evasion, slander and stratagem, until Othello finally demands "ocular proof" and Iago produces the incriminating handkerchief.

Iago is master of the situation in the beginning, and his mastery is built on his knowledge of Othello's character. Yet that knowledge is inadequate. Iago perceives that

> *The Moor is of a free and open nature,*
> *That thinks men honest that but seem to be so, . . .*

but he is not aware of the torrent of passion which, once aroused, Othello can unleash. It is Iago's intention to center his ingenuity on Cassio, whose death would satisfy his purpose; but Desdemona must be involved to complete the proof of Cassio's guilt; in injuring Desdemona's reputation Cassio will filch from Othello his good name. Iago's plan does not at first include Desdemona's death; his plea at the end of the third act, "But let her live," probably means just that.[22] However, he overshoots his mark; Othello insists upon death for both Cassio and Desdemona, and the scene closes with Iago's ironically submissive line, "I am your own for ever."

But Iago has not reckoned with the primitive power of passion smouldering in the Moor—to be released later when he is aroused by sexual jealousy. For the remainder of the play Iago is influenced by Othello's passion more than Othello by Iago's intrigue.[23] Iago becomes more and more deeply involved. Roderigo's failure to kill Cassio initiates Iago's ill luck, which terminates at last in his wife's impassioned revelation of his villainy.

During the course of his designs it is necessary that Iago's apparent honesty be plausible in order that Othello's credulity—his failure to suspect Iago, his inability to penetrate the villain's purpose—may not be a weakness too seriously impugning his character. Hence, Iago's reputation for integrity is made credible not only to the trusting Othello but also to everyone else in the play, even to his wife, until the last scene. Indeed, Iago's reputation for honesty becomes an ironic motif. The word "honest," repeatedly introduced with reference to Iago, and sometimes with reference to Desdemona, fluctuates in meaning between "honorable" and "chaste."[24]

49

Iago hates nobility in human nature. His base conception of mankind he expresses in animal imagery. He has contempt for the world of Othello and Desdemona and no conception of the spirituality of their love. Cynically he regards such love as mere lust, a "sanctimony and a frail vow betwixt an erring barbarian and a super-subtle Venetian."

But even the skill of Iago could not have succeeded in overcoming Othello if there had not been latent in Othello's character a weakness for the villain to play upon. And yet, at the beginning Othello shows no trace of such weakness. Othello's self-mastery, tested on the field of battle, is complete. He stands firm in the confidence of a glorious past, "loving his own pride and purposes," as Iago ironically says. The black Moorish general in the employ of the Venetian state is a man with manifest pride in his military achievements. He is aware of his high merit which, without boasting, he expects the world to recognize. Called before the Venetian senate to explain his elopement with Desdemona, to answer the charge of "witchcraft" brought by his wife's enraged father, Othello is courteous and dignified in his expression of restrained affection. Though little accustomed to words, in an eloquent speech he recounts frankly the story of his courtship. Othello is master of every passion. He asks the indulgence of the senators in Desdemona's wish to accompany him to Cyprus, not to "please the palate of my appetite" but "to be free and bounteous to her mind." And when the senate commands him to depart on his wedding night, he answers unhesitatingly, "With all my heart."

In the first act Othello is content because he is dependent only upon himself. Because he has been engaged in military affairs wherein he himself is primarily concerned, he is unperturbed. But at the beginning of the second act, after the tempestuous voyage, Othello is no longer the "noble Moor whom our full senate call all in all sufficient." He has been transmuted by his love for Desdemona, and upon his re-union at Cyprus he realizes that a great share of his content comes from his happiness in his young Venetian wife. He addresses his "fair warrior":

> *If it were now to die,*
> *'Twere now to be most happy; for, I fear,*
> *My soul hath her content so absolute*
> *That not another comfort like to this*
> *Succeeds in unknown fate.*

The new relationship presents difficulties which Othello has not previously encountered, and which his pride in military matters can lead him to underestimate. Othello's idealizing love fills him with tenderness toward the "gentle" Desdemona. Emotion excites his imagination to poetic utterance. His is the selfishness of romantic love, while Desdemona's is the selflessness of realistic passion. And in the disparity of their love lies a source of danger for both.[25] Othello, in the story of his courtship told to the senate in the first act, has summed up their mutual affection:

> *She lov'd me for the dangers I had pass'd,*
> *And I lov'd her that she did pity them.*

But Desdemona had boldly declared,

> *That I did love the Moor to live with him,*
> *My downright violence and storm of fortunes*
> *May trumpet to the world.*

The significance of Desdemona's full, strong, sexual passion is not apparent to Othello, nor does he realize the depth of her mature confession: "I saw Othello's visage in his mind. . . ." Although Desdemona is Othello's world, in which, as he says,

> *I have garner'd up my heart,*
> *Where either I must live or bear no life,*

his imperfect understanding of his wife's love is a source of as great danger to him as Iago's villainy; indeed, if Othello had maintained complete confidence in his wife's loyalty Iago's cunning would not have been effective.

The gulf between the Moor and his Venetian wife is a barrier which Othello's inadequate sensibility cannot bridge. But this barrier is not at first apparent. The duke and the senate at the beginning, Lodovico and Gratiano at the end of the tragedy, show the Moor only admiration and treat the marriage as above reproach. But Brabantio, who had earlier lionized the Moor at his home, is now aroused by his daughter's elopement and condemns the Moor for his color. And later the shrewd Iago urges the disparities of race, color, and rank as insuperable obstructions to a happy marriage.

Nevertheless, difference in sensibility is a barrier not only for the Moor who, aroused, is "perplex'd in the extreme," but also for Desdemona, who fails to understand his passion. Desdemona's failure to understand is due to her lack of worldly knowledge. Desdemona, who could have checked Othello's mounting suspicion had she recognized its nature, only intensifies his passion by her social naïveté. She is far from the "cunning whore of Venice" that Othello supposes her. The thought of women who betray their husbands is beyond her comprehension. Indeed, in her bewilderment, she declares, "I cannot say 'whore.'" Desdemona is good not in spite of temptation to be otherwise but because she knows evil only by name. Although she had strength to defy convention in marrying Othello and to oppose her father's fury before the senate in supporting her husband, her actions thereafter tend only toward her downfall. Lack of understanding of her husband leads to her imprudent pressing of Cassio's suit and later to her denial of the loss of the handkerchief in an effort to mollify her husband's wrath. The same "gentleness" of nature characterizes her when she speaks falsely in her dying breath to save her murderer, her "kind lord." Desdemona's death is consequently the pathos of innocent suffering.

Crazed with passion, Othello is thoroughly persuaded that his wife is a "subtle whore." He is resolved upon personal vindication as satisfaction for his "discarded" love and as retaliation for the humiliation of being made the laughing stock of society,[26]

> The fixed figure for the time of scorn
> To point his slow and moving finger at!

Othello resolves in the office of just avenger to stifle his wife. He further conceives of himself as fulfilling a higher duty: he will remove from society a source of infection, "else she'll betray more men." Desdemona, whose beauty had seemed to him the embodiment of purity, now seems a source of defilement. He approaches his task with a tone of mercy, asking Desdemona to confess her sins, for he would not kill her soul. Her denial of guilt as well as her plea for mercy infuriates Othello and, as he says,

> ...makes me call what I intend to do
> A murder, which I thought a sacrifice.

Conceiving of himself as an agent of divine justice, he

murders Desdemona in a fit of rage, even before she has had time to say "one prayer." The mercy which his dying wife extends in an effort to exonerate her husband, he cannot accept:

> She's, like a liar, gone to burning hell.
> 'Twas I that kill'd her.

The revelation of Emilia informs Othello not only against Iago but also against himself. He repents, and looking at his dead wife's innocence cries,

> ... when we shall meet at compt,
> This look of thine will hurl my soul from heaven,
> And fiends will snatch at it.

Thoughts of the last judgment cause Othello to judge himself. In his self-subduing knowledge he realizes the entirety of Desdemona's love, as well as the limitations of a man who, failing to grasp the strength of his wife's fidelity, "lov'd not wisely but too well." In his final moments he recovers his essential nobility and recognizes Desdemona's inmost as well as her outward beauty. His suicide is an atonement for an act done in the ignorance of passion.

Shakespeare, like Sophocles, is in the end concerned that evil shall not dominate the scene. In *Othello* a punishment for Iago is designed—one which "can torment him much and hold him long." Justice is done the reputation of Othello in this world by his own acknowledgment, in the speech asseverating, "I have done the state some service," and in Cassio's final pronouncement, "For he was great of heart."

In neither *Oedipus the King* nor *Othello* is there a justification of the ways of god to man in the sense in which

Aeschylus presents such a reconciliation.[27] Yet in the case of each hero there appears a revelation of character superior to overpowering circumstances—an ironic and inexplicable likeness to life, in the Aristotelian sense.

Oedipus at Colonus and King Lear

Oedipus at Colonus

IT SEEMS that Sophocles wrote *Oedipus at Colonus* to vindicate the character of Oedipus, for Oedipus here protests that his motives were pure and that he erred unwittingly, and his plea will be substantiated at the end of the tragedy.

About twenty years have elapsed since the close of *Oedipus the King*, and we see the king a blind beggar, exiled and cityless, the "ghost of him who once was Oedipus," leaning for protection on his daughter Antigone, who herself needs protection. From scattered details in *Oedipus at Colonus* we learn that Oedipus was first detained at Thebes against his will. But when time had calmed his mood the Thebans demanded his expulsion because it was felt that the city was harboring a defilement, and Creon yielded. It is significant that no oracle is mentioned as the cause of his exile. Oedipus blames Thebes solely, for neither his two sons nor Creon spoke a word to arrest his expulsion. His two daughters are loyal: Antigone accompanies her father in his wanderings, and Ismene remains at Thebes to observe the course of events there in her father's interest. Ismene brings the latest oracle from Thebes and interprets to her father its purport, that some day the Thebans invading Athens will be routed in a battle near the grave of Oedipus, for Apollo has foretold that the

tomb of Oedipus, a legacy to Athens, will bring a curse on Thebes. "The gods, who once abased, uplift thee now," says Ismene.

The character of Oedipus in *Oedipus at Colonus* remains firm in spite of age and suffering; Oedipus' old fiery temper is only smouldering, ready to blaze forth when aroused. Presently Creon enters—an emissary from Thebes for the purpose of securing the person of Oedipus, whose tomb, according to the oracle, will have power for victory. The insolent solicitations of Creon, backed by threats and force, kindle the ire of Oedipus. Hearing the outcry, Theseus, king of Athens, rushes to the scene.

Creon tries to convince Theseus that he would have desisted had not Oedipus' anger provoked him:

> *I had refrained but for the curses dire*
> *Wherewith he banned my kinsfolk and myself:*
> *Such wrong, methought, had warrant for my act.*

But Oedipus detects Creon's duplicity:

> *Thou art come to take me, not to take me home,*
> *But plant me on thy borders, that thy State*
> *May so escape annoyance from this land.*

Creon is here a villain, unlike the Creon of *Oedipus the King*. But Theseus attributes his changed attitude to dotage when he tells him:

> *. . . plenitude of years*
> *Have made of thee an old man and a fool.*

Creon, a rival of Theseus for the possession of the outcast Oedipus, by his effrontery places the magnanimity of the Attic hero in strong relief. It is noteworthy that men of base nature are seldom introduced in Sophocles; Creon is an exception.

Oedipus' temper again flames out when his older son, Polyneices, begs assistance in a military effort to regain the throne of Thebes from a younger brother, Eteocles; for according to the oracle, victory will fall to the side which has Oedipus for ally. Oedipus answers Polyneices' appeal for sympathy:

> *O villain, when thou hadst the sovereignty*
> *That now thy brother holdeth in thy stead,*
> *Didst thou not drive me, thine own father, out,*
> *An exile, cityless, and make me wear*
> *This beggar's garb thou weepest to behold,*
> *Now thou art come thyself to my sad plight?*

Oedipus remains unyielding to the end. He leaves his son a curse as his last bequest—a curse which is later fulfilled:

> *Never to win by arms thy native land,*
> *No, nor return to Argos in the Vale,*
> *But by a kinsman's hand to die and slay*
> *Him who expelled thee.*

The movement of plot in *Oedipus at Colonus* is the reverse of the movement in *Oedipus the King*. In the latter play Oedipus is cast down from a height of unusual eminence; in *Oedipus at Colonus* his lot moves from humility to exaltation.[28] Oedipus will be honored in his death, for he is destined to become one of Attica's tutelary heroes. His kingship in Thebes was only apparent majesty; his true majesty is revealed when the Eumenides permit him to set foot in their awful grove on ground too sacred for human foot to tread, and when Theseus, the hero-king of Athens, gives him welcome, and he answers:

I come to offer thee this woe-worn frame,
A gift not fair to look on; yet its worth
More precious far than any outward show.

At the end of the tragedy Oedipus' passion has subsided, leaving him resigned and content. He feels himself endued with mystic power, and reserved by the gods for the accomplishment of their purpose—his own vindication and the saving of Athens. Athens, which received him when the rest of the world rejected him, will find safety from his tomb. The elevation to which Oedipus has been raised by his apparent fall is dramatically symbolized by his exaltation above his blind dependence when suddenly the triple sounds of thunder, signifying divine approval, summon him, and he leads the way, guide of his former guides, to the place appointed for his tomb. A messenger reports his death:

For without wailing or disease or pain
He passed away—an end most marvellous.

To leave the mystery unbroken, Theseus, who alone was permitted to observe his passing, bowed down and kissed the earth, then rose and stretched out his hands to the sky. The vision which he had just seen moved him to reverence the deities of both worlds.

Oedipus at Colonus is a religious and patriotic mystery. The audience is left with the feeling that Oedipus' tragic life was not without purpose and that the honor which awaited him makes posthumous amends for his undeserved suffering. The emotions aroused in the drama are allayed, the dissonance proceeds to consonance, and the tragedy ends in a tonic chord, in a harmony of the will of Oedipus with that of the divine.[29]

King Lear

THE ennobling effect of suffering in which character is
superior to circumstances is the essence of the tragedy in
both *Oedipus at Colonus* and *King Lear*. Oedipus, former
king of Thebes, wanders, a blind and banished beggar, in
Athens; Lear, stripped of the attributes of kingship, ejected
by his daughters, wanders exposed to the elements on the
heath. Because of the stout resistance to suffering displayed
by both Oedipus and Lear, that which might be considered
the pathos of the infirmity of age becomes poetic irony.

A minor theme of both tragedies is filial ingratitude.
Oedipus' sons make no move to stay his banishment, and
Lear's older daughters are finally responsible for their
father's expulsion. But while the theme of filial ingratitude
occurs in the plays (as also in the Gloucester plot of *King
Lear*), the theme of filial gratitude is present also. Oedipus
is befriended in his exile by his daughters Antigone and
Ismene, and Lear is received in the end by Cordelia, the
daughter he had disinherited.

It has sometimes been objected that *King Lear*, like
Oedipus the King, is based upon improbabilities. It is
argued that it is absurd to base a tragedy either on the
patricide and incest of Oedipus or upon the apportionment
of a kingdom in accordance with three daughters' profes-
sions of filial affection, as in *King Lear*. Aristotle justifies
the improbability in *Oedipus the King* on the grounds that
it lies outside the action of the plot, and very likely he
would have made allowances for *King Lear* in some such
way as Coleridge has done. Coleridge insists, "Let the first
scene of *Lear* have been lost, and let it be only understood
that a fond father had been duped by hypocritical pro-
fessions of love and duty on the part of two daughters

to disinherit a third, previously, and deservedly, more dear to him, and all the rest of the tragedy would retain its interest undiminished, and be perfectly intelligible."[30] In both tragedies, once the improbabilities are assumed, the action follows as a result of character. The improbable events are comparable to circumstances in life which we are forced to accept but for which we can find no justification.

Aristotle's ideal tragedy requires a character predominantly good, though not perfect; and it is noteworthy that the imperfection in the character of many Greek and Shakespearean protagonists is rashness of judgment. It is Lear's rashness that impels him to disinherit Cordelia and to banish Kent, and thus to initiate his downfall. Lear's hasty temper is shown most violently in his invocation of the curse of childlessness upon Goneril, and Oedipus' temper is most conspicuously displayed in his invocation of the curse of death upon his hypocritical son Polyneices.

That Lear is in part responsible for his disaster cannot be denied. Had he been less impetuous in the rejection of his youngest daughter, had he gone to live with Cordelia as he purposed, there would have been no tragedy of Lear. But it would please the old king's pride to hear his daughters profess their affection for him openly. As both feudal king and autocratic father he is accustomed to fealty. Cordelia's apparent defiance when asked what she has to say —"Nothing"—arouses the king. Because he loves Cordelia most deeply, he feels her bluntness most keenly. Had Cordelia indulged her father's whim, she might have escaped his hasty judgment. But it is significant that Cordelia is reacting against the hypocrisy of her sisters. Out of her solicitude for her father she would denounce their "glib and oily art." Her assertion that she cannot give her father all her love, that half is due a husband, is reminiscent of Desdemona's and Juliet's choice of duty to husband.

Cordelia's answer to her father is defended by the king of France, who takes her dowerless as his wife. But, more significantly, it is Kent who comes to her defense—the blunt, old, honest Kent, staunchly loyal to his sovereign Lear—who can affirm,

> *My life I never held but as a pawn*
> *To wage against thine enemies, . . .*

and who, after he has been banished by the king for his determination to speak out, can return in disguise to serve his master, in whose face he recognizes "authority."

No sooner has the "old kind king" divided his kingdom between his two daughters than the two daughters perceive trouble from his "unconstant starts," authoritative outbursts such as led him to banish Kent. Goneril and Regan agree that they will tolerate none of his autocracy, which the infirmity of age has aggravated. Lear, however, while wishing to unburden himself of the cares of kingship, would remain "every inch a king," for he would retain "the name, and all th' addition to a king," as well as his hundred riotous retainers to whose revels Goneril and Regan object. Goneril is accordingly ready to "disquantity" his train before he has remained with her the allotted month. Lear now begins to perceive the purpose of Goneril's effusive profession of love, and in the light of her hypocrisy he understands more fully Cordelia's blunt assertion, when he affirms:

> *O most small fault,*
> *How ugly didst thou in Cordelia show!*

Enraged by his daughter's ingratitude, "sharper than a

61

serpent's tooth," Lear pronounces a curse on Goneril.

In rising wrath, Lear begins to weep, and is ashamed of his unmanliness. Frequently during the course of the action Lear attempts to control his anger and his tears. He withholds his angry tears in the presence of Regan, who would further reduce his train. "Patience," he cries repeatedly in an effort to steel himself, before his wits stray and he wanders delirious on the heath. At the end of the tragedy, when Lear realizes Cordelia is dead, he has recovered his manliness and is beyond the need of tears.

Lear's suffering has given him a wider sympathy with mankind. In the tempest on the heath, after he has sent the Fool to shelter, he prays:

> *Poor naked wretches, wheresoe'er you are,*
> *That bide the pelting of this pitiless storm,*
> *How shall your houseless heads and unfed sides,*
> *Your loop'd and window'd raggedness, defend you*
> *From seasons such as these? O, I have ta'en*
> *Too little care of this!*

His encounter with Edgar, disguised as the madman Poor Tom, provokes his further pity: "Is man no more than this?" Lear can endure no more. His wits stray, and, tearing off his garments, emblems of royal prerogatives, he strips himself not only of the responsibility but also of the protection due a king. With head exposed to the elements, he feels in his defenselessness a pity for innocent sufferers in the world.[31]

Lear's restoration to Cordelia marks the height of his joy and the triumph of his effort to gain "patience," for he can now bend to ask her forgiveness and find content in her presence. With her he feels he could be happy even in prison, for to him the world has become a thing of indifference.

But ironically his happiness is brief, for in Cordelia's death Lear loses all. When he brings her body onto the stage he holds a feather to her lips in the hope that she still lives, and observes:

> *If it be so,*
> *It is a chance which does redeem all sorrows*
> *That ever I have felt.*

Grief over Cordelia's death bows the old king so that he fails to comprehend fully even the devotion of Kent, who now reveals himself. He dies during Kent's entreaty:

> *...O, let him pass! He hates him*
> *That would upon the rack of this tough world*
> *Stretch him out longer.*

At the end of the tragedy, it is a group of good characters which survives. In the major plot, even though Lear and Cordelia perish, Kent and Albany remain; in the minor plot, although Gloucester dies, Edgar remains to carry on the rule. All the evil characters perish: Goneril, Regan, Cornwall, and Oswald in the major plot, and in the minor plot the bastard son Edmund. Finally, order is restored and arrangement is made for amity in the state.

Justice is done so far as is humanly possible, and, as in *Oedipus at Colonus*, there is a resolution of discords in harmony. Albany's final tribute to Lear's noble endurance of suffering is fitting also for Oedipus:

> *The oldest hath borne most; we that are young*
> *Shall never see so much, nor live so long.*

Antigone and *Hamlet*

Antigone

ALTHOUGH Sophocles wrote *Antigone* before he wrote the Oedipus plays, the story of Antigone is a continuation of the story of the house of Labdacus in another generation. Antigone has returned to Thebes. She has seen her brothers die in mutual fratricide when the city from which Eteocles had expelled his older brother Polyneices was besieged by Polyneices and his Argive allies. The seven leaders of the Argive enemy have been slain at the gates of the city by as many Theban chiefs, and, deprived of its commanders, the Argive army has fled. Creon, uncle of the slain sons of Oedipus, now rules in Thebes. The scene is laid before the palace of Creon, once the palace of Oedipus. Creon has pronounced an edict that the body of Eteocles, the patriot, shall be honorably buried, but that the corpse of the traitor Polyneices shall be left on the plain outside the city walls for dogs and crows to mangle.

The character of Antigone here is a consistent development of that in *Oedipus at Colonus*.[32] In *Oedipus at Colonus* Sophocles shows Antigone's unselfish devotion to her old, blind father in his wanderings and reproaches, and her depth of familial affection in her anxiety to reconcile her warring brothers and to save them from the curse invoked by their father. In *Oedipus at Colonus* Polyneices, anticipating the fulfillment of his father's curse, has begged his sisters:

> *My sisters, ye his daughters, ye have heard*
> *The prayers of our stern father, if his curse*
> *Should come to pass and ye some day return*

To Thebes, O then disown me not, I pray,
But grant me burial and due funeral rites.

In the opening scene of *Antigone* the curse is shown to
be fulfilled, and Antigone is indignant that her brother has
been denied burial. She resolves to bury Polyneices in defiance of the king's command. Her resolve to disobey the
royal edict is prompted by her sense of duty to both her
brother and the gods below.

Ismene attempts to dissuade her defiant sister by com-
mending the course of reason. Ismene acts as a foil to the
passionate Antigone.[33] Antigone, finding in her sister's ir-
resolution no aid, defies Creon and sets forth to do the
deed alone, although she knows that death is the penalty.
By sprinkling handfuls of dust and pouring libations on
the corpse, Antigone gives Polyneices symbolic burial and
thus saves her brother the dishonor which would otherwise
have befallen him in the other world. In according him
burial, she has discharged her duty to the gods below as
well as to Polyneices, for such duty devolves upon the
nearest living relative.[34] But by violating the edict of the
state she has also incurred the ire of Creon.

Creon argues the reasons for unquestioning obedience to
the state. He earnestly believes that it is his duty as ruler
to enforce obedience, because the safety of the individual
depends upon the safety of the state. Moreover, obedience
must be absolute, for he says:

Whome'er the State
Appoints, must be obeyed in everything,
Both small and great, just and unjust alike.

Creon argues that if the individual presumes to decide for

himself which laws to obey, there will be anarchy. He therefore concludes that he must curb disobedience by punishment—nor does he believe that the gods will uphold a disloyal citizen.

The chorus of Theban counsellors, at this point, thinks that Antigone acted foolishly in disobeying the edict; the law should remain inviolate—although they consider the decree an error.

Antigone affirms that the people of Thebes believe she did a glorious deed, and argues:

> *Nor did I deem that thou, a mortal man,*
> *Could'st by a breath annul and override*
> *The immutable unwritten laws of Heaven.*

Creon's son, Haemon, betrothed to Antigone, corroborates Antigone's affirmation. Calmly at first, Haemon pleads Antigone's case with an appeal to his father's reputation as a just king—one who listens to the advice of others, unless he is omniscient. Finding his case hopeless, and stung by his father's taunts, Haemon lashes out with rebukes and threatens to destroy himself should Antigone perish. It is significant that Antigone and Haemon do not appear together in a scene; by keeping the two apart Sophocles emphasizes in the tragedy Antigone's paramount purpose to perform a sacred duty as against her desire for earthly happiness with Haemon.[35]

It might be mentioned here that the guard who apprehended Antigone was another of her sympathizers. He had pity for her, but not as much pity as he would have felt for himself had he failed to apprehend her![36]

But it is Teiresias, the seer, who convinces the counsellors that Creon is wrong in enforcing the edict, and the counsel-

lors at length persuade Creon. Teiresias perceives that disobedience to an arbitrary decree of a tyrant is not disloyalty
to the state, for he tells Creon, "... thou usurp'st a power
not thine." Although Creon's intentions are good, his mind
can grasp only the letter of the law.[37] Nevertheless, it
should be noted that Creon had misgivings about im-
prisoning Antigone; his uncertainty was especially evident
in his furious reproaches against the counsellors, against
Haemon, and finally against the seer who, angered by the
king, threatened divine retribution.[38] Creon yields at last
to the counsel of the chorus. He will release Antigone from
her rock tomb, where she has been immured with food
sufficient only to avert the pollution that would fall upon
the state on account of death by starvation.[39]

Creon relents, but for Antigone there is no yielding. The
dilemma involving choice of duty to the state or duty to
the divine law left her only the choice of the higher loyalty.
Having sternly rejected Ismene's second-thought offer to
share responsibility for the deed, and by her inflexible truth-
fulness having convinced Creon that Ismene was not an
accomplice, Antigone now stands alone. She turns for pity
to the chorus of the opposite sex, but theirs is mock comfort: they attempt to console her with thoughts of posthumous fame. Dying unwed and before her allotted life
is spent, Antigone questions momentarily the wisdom of
her act: in the earlier exaltation of action she had not
paused to think.[40] She sees clearly the disastrous result of
doing right. She is to die in the discharge of a sacred duty.
Life is dear to her, yet ironically her reward is death.

But Creon has been persuaded to save her. The chorus,
rejoicing over Creon's change of mind, sings a *hyporcheme*
just before the messenger enters to announce the double

suicide. Because he stops to perform the burial rites for Polyneices, Creon arrives at the tomb too late to save Antigone[41]—or his son Haemon. Haemon, after an affront to his father with the drawn sword, has committed suicide in remorse for Antigone's death.

Antigone has faint hope that she will be vindicated in another world. (Tragedy, to the Greek, occurs in this world, not in the next.) Viewed from the standpoint of the individual, Antigone suffers in excess of her deserts. In such suffering there is poetic irony, even though Antigone's death assists in the vindication of the moral order.

To Creon, acknowledging his responsibility for Haemon's death, and humbled after his *hybris*, a messenger brings news of his wife Eurydice's suicide on account of grief for her son. The messenger adds that Eurydice died cursing her husband both for her own death and for her son's. And the chorus reminds the anguish-stricken king that it is dangerous to defy the will of the gods, but that wisdom comes through suffering.

Hamlet

> *The time is out of joint;—O cursed spite,*
> *That ever I was born to set it right!*

cries Hamlet, when he discovers the duty imposed upon him, and Antigone might well have echoed the thought. At the opening of the Shakespearean and Sophoclean tragedies, two young idealists lament the obligations thrust upon them by a world of astonishing evil. For Hamlet that evil world is represented by his uncle Claudius; for Antigone the evil is embodied in her uncle Creon. Hamlet is compelled to act because he cannot leave his father unavenged; Antigone, because she cannot leave her brother unburied. In both plays it is the character of the protagonists which commands the main interest, and it is the nobility of their nature which gives distinction to the tragedies. For the protagonists, the reward for heroism is ultimately disillusionment and death.

When *Hamlet* opens, the prince of Denmark is introduced as a highly sensitive youth, in despair over the death of a father whom he worshiped and the hasty marriage, "within a month," of his mother. Because he is so finely tuned, his mother's "incestuous" marriage—her disloyalty to the ideal embodied in his father—so much offends him. His depth of despair is revealed in a soliloquy expressing a wish for death:

> *O, that this too too solid flesh would melt,*
> *Thaw, and resolve itself into a dew!*
> *Or that the Everlasting had not fix'd*
> *His canon 'gainst self-slaughter! O God! God!*
> *How weary, stale, flat, and unprofitable,*
> *Seems to me all the uses of this world!*

To Hamlet's disillusioned and depressed mind the ghost of his father addresses the injunction, "Revenge his foul and most unnatural murder." Hamlet has misgivings about the authenticity of the ghost until his doubts are removed by the blenching of the king in the mouse-trap scene. But he does not question the morality of the murder; the murder is divinely appointed.

At this point it might be mentioned that although the practice of murder for the sake of revenge was no longer condoned at the time of Aeschylus' writing of the *Oresteia*, dramatists continued to use the revenge motif as a basis for tragedy. From the Greeks, significantly through the tragedies of the Seneca, the revenge motif passed into Elizabethan tragedy.

The many murders that ensue in the course of fulfillment of the supernatural command, the prince feels are enforced upon him. The accidental stabbing of Polonius he regrets, but he excuses himself:

> *I do repent; but Heaven hath pleas'd it so,*
> *To punish me with this and this with me,*
> *That I must be their scourge and minister.*

Like the autocratic Creon in *Antigone*, Claudius is the chief enemy. And Claudius is no ordinary villain. The urbane, diplomatic king would willingly live in peace with his nephew and take him as son and heir. Moreover, Claudius would repent of his recent fratricide; he prays for forgiveness. But he finds he cannot repent because he retains all the attributes of his stolen kingship—the crown, the queen, and his own ambition.

While the king is in the act of prayer, Hamlet has opportunity to kill him. However, in accordance with a principle of revenge tragedy the blow may be greater but not less than the injury.[42] Since Claudius destroyed the elder Hamlet with all his imperfections on his head, as the "beauteous majesty of Denmark" has revealed, Hamlet feels he would not be revenged if he took the king in the act of purging his soul—he must kill both body and soul.[43] He spares the king when he discovers him on his knees, although the king is ironically unable to purge his soul by prayer.

Hamlet finally gets his revenge when he stabs the king. Nor would Hamlet's supporters have wished it otherwise.

Hamlet throughout the play is popular with the people, even as is Antigone (whose cause was urged by Haemon, representing *vox populi*, by Teiresias threatening divine retribution, and finally by the chorus of counsellors persuading Creon to submit). Claudius hesitates to destroy Hamlet openly because of "the great love the general gender bear him"—although he feels he might instigate Hamlet's destruction secretly because the prince is "generous and free from all contriving." Ophelia, who should know, early summarizes his princely virtues:

> The courtier's, soldier's, scholar's, eye, tongue, sword;
> The expectancy and rose of the fair state....

The queen loves Hamlet too well to betray his confidence, and Horatio would drain the cup of poison to die with him. Fortinbras perceives that this son of a warrior father would have been a worthy ruler and gives him burial "like a soldier."

And yet, in spite of the human sympathy with which Hamlet and Antigone are surrounded, each is curiously isolated from his fellows in the accomplishment of his purpose. The love theme in both plays is minor. Only in death can Haemon share Antigone's rock-hewn prison, and only in madness can Ophelia enter Hamlet's antic world— even though Haemon seeks union with his betrothed in suicide and Hamlet momentarily joins Ophelia in the grave of her "doubtful" death. Nor does a boon companion offer much greater comfort. Ismene is early rejected by Antigone. Horatio, the voice of reason, though an understanding foil for the hero throughout the play, does not become an accomplice in the murder of Claudius. In the end he acts only as a messenger from the dead.

It is with the clearing of his reputation that Hamlet is chiefly concerned in the end. Denmark is to know why he killed his uncle, the king. Horatio is to tell that which has been untold, the story of the murder of the elder Hamlet and the ghostly mandate to revenge. Ironically, the ordnance that celebrated the king's triumphal wassail now signalizes Hamlet's burial.[44] The king has taken his final rouse, this time from his nephew's cup, and Hamlet in death achieves an ironic triumph.

Frequently, in each play, a paean to the power and dignity of mankind has been discovered. Less frequently have the words about misuse of that power been noted. A beautiful choral song in *Antigone* mingles admiration of man's ingenuity with misgivings about his use of it:

> *Many wonders there be, but naught more*
> *wondrous than man:*
> . . . .
> *Passing the wildest flight of thought are the*
> *cunning and skill,*
> *That guide man now to the light, but now to*
> *counsels of ill.*

Among the many passages in *Hamlet* expressing the height and depth of human endeavor, one might be selected:

What a piece of work is a man! How noble in reason! How infinite in faculty, in form and moving! How express and admirable in action! How like an angel in apprehension! How like a god! The beauty of the world! The paragon of animals! And yet, to me, what is this quintessence of dust?

Later, in the gravemakers' scene, Hamlet holds in his hand the skull of a king's jester and reflects that to this "favour" must we all come—king and clown, Alexander and Yorick.

Both tragedies close with the restoration of justice to the state. Creon, overcome by his personal losses, is now ready to abandon his arbitrary rule. He longs for death. In Denmark the usurping brother of the elder Hamlet will be succeeded by Fortinbras, a leader chosen by the dying voice of the younger Hamlet.

And what of justice to the individual? From one point of view, the destruction of Hamlet and Antigone seems a pitiful waste of excellence in a world where well-meaning human effort leads to death.[45] Both die in an effort to uphold what seems to them a higher law than that of the state. Although Antigone has some doubt of her vindication in another world, she is sure she is right so far as justice in this world is concerned. After summarizing her part in honors paid the family dead, she apostrophizes her "traitor" brother:

> And last, my Polyneices, unto thee
> I paid due rites, and this my recompense!
> Yet am I justified in wisdom's eyes.

Hamlet, finally, is no longer concerned about whether he is "to be, or not to be . . ." in another world. He has come to the conclusion that "there's a special providence in the fall of a sparrow." In the light of some distant, divine plan he finds comfort—

> There's a divinity that shapes our ends,
> Rough-hew them how we will . . .

—and he discovers some compensation for suffering in the knowledge that "the readiness is all." In this connection, Greene's remarks are enlightening: "For the supreme compensation for suffering lies in its educative power. Man learns, first, that he has unsuspected powers of passive endurance.... He learns, too, that his will is free; his motives may still be pure, whatever the fell hand of circumstance may bring.... Finally, over and above the potentialities of a noble nature, the product of inheritance ... and aristocratic training, there is the personal code of the hero, his sense of honor or *arete*, which gains strength with demands that are made on it, and which knows no compromise with lesser loyalties, or even with fate."[46] At this point Aristotle, too, has something to say: "Yet nevertheless even in adversity nobility shines through, when a man endures repeated and severe misfortune with patience, not owing to insensibility but from generosity and greatness of soul."[47]

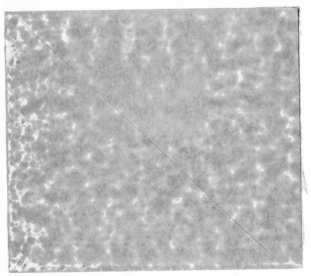

FOUR

PATHOS

ALTHOUGH Aristotle reserves his highest praise for Sophocles, he praises Euripides as the "most tragic of the poets,"[1] perhaps because Euripides, in his dramas which may most aptly be called tragedies, stresses the pathos of human suffering at the hands of capricious divinities.[2]

The Greek word *pathos* may refer to the emotions themselves, such as love and hate, but it is here used with reference to a type of *ethos* based more on noble feeling than on noble acting. Although pathos may be viewed as a kind of irony, the emphasis is rather on the malignity of the circumstances than on the character of the protagonist and the importance of his moral choices. Pathos, as it appears in Euripides' *Hippolytus* and in Shakespeare's *Romeo and Juliet*, is the result of unmerited suffering of admirable human beings confronted by adverse circumstances for which they are little responsible and which they cannot overcome.

Euripides' tragedies illustrate the injustice of undeserved suffering on the part of noble but defeated human beings. Sophocles, though equally concerned with the ruthlessness of natural forces, stresses the nobility of imperfect human nature encountering disaster not altogether undeserved. In Euripides' *Hippolytus* the element of pity is overwhelming; but one is disposed to wonder whether the element of

fear is sufficiently aroused, whether the spectator can identify himself with a protagonist so predominantly good.
Butcher observes: "The requirement of Aristotle is pity
and fear. He would no doubt allow that in some tragedies
the primary and predominant impression is fear, in others
pity. He would probably go farther and say that an inferior
tragedy may excite one only of the two emotions generally
called tragic. But the full tragic effect requires the union
of the two, nor can the distinctive function of tragedy as
katharsis be discharged otherwise."[3] Euripides, making his
dramatic action turn on inability to overcome misfortune,
found it difficult to induce tragic pity from the spectacle
of the hero's suffering.

Sophocles' idealistic representation of "men as they ought
to be" appealed more to the contemporary Athenian audience than did Euripides' realistic portrayal of men "as they
are."[4] It is a commentary upon the judgment of the audience of Periclean Athens that they awarded the prize in
dramatic competition far more frequently to Sophocles than
to Euripides, although Euripides during his lifetime was
popular with the younger Athenians and received his laurels
posthumously.

Hippolytus and *Romeo and Juliet*

Hippolytus

THERE was a period of thirty years between the production
of Aeschylus' *Oresteia* in 458 B.C. and Euripides' *Hippolytus* in 428 B.C. In those three decades the conception of
man's tragic nature when placed in opposition to external
forces had changed markedly. As has been said, Aeschylus
in his most mature work conceived of a universe in which

rewards and punishments are allotted by divine powers in accordance with man's deserts. Sophocles emphasized the nobility of man's nature when confronted by insuperable odds and conceived of tragedy as the ironic discrepancy between man's suffering and his deserts, thus explaining though not justifying undeserved misfortune. Euripides, in his dramas which best represent his tragic idea of life, *Hippolytus* and the *Bacchae*, conceives of human nature as destroyed unjustly by forces with which it is unable to cope.

The tragic view of Euripides represents man, who uses reason, preyed on by irrational forces. In *Hippolytus* the irrational is symbolized by the goddess Aphrodite operating through human agents, Phaedra and Theseus, to effect the downfall of Hippolytus; in the *Bacchae* Pentheus, a symbol of rationality, is overcome by the emotional force embodied in the god Dionysus. Nevertheless, Euripides does not disparage utterly such emotional forces as are embodied in Aphrodite and Dionysus.

Sophocles and Euripides were competitors throughout their dramatic careers in the City Dionysia. While both wrote on themes chosen from the old myths, Sophocles generally upheld the sanctity of the divine laws, while Euripides taught his audience to question the incompatibilities of the traditional religion. The conclusion of *Oedipus at Colonus* and that of *Hippolytus* illustrate the religious difference between Sophocles and Euripides.

Yet Euripides, like Aeschylus, sought to reform the Olympic pantheon. And even though the national religion had been largely supplanted by skepticism at the time of Euripides, Euripides accepted the old myths for dramatic purposes, at the same time impugning the justice of the gods in their treatment of human beings.

Because Euripides constantly criticizes the gods while at the same time he uses them as forces in his tragedies, his conception of the gods results in an ambiguity. Euripides sees the gods both as they ought to be and as they seem to be. He offers no resolution of the problem. Greene asserts: "Between these extremes of faith and doubt it is the business of religion to mediate. But Euripides cannot be said to have found any reconciliation between the cosmic and the moral laws. The gods and the myths he has accepted for dramatic purposes, even to the extent of sometimes using the gods in final scenes to give a pious conclusion to a story that offends the moral sense."[5]

In *Hippolytus* Euripides reveals the gods as powers contributing to the pathos of man's misfortune. The gods should be wiser than men, says the servant in *Hippolytus,* but Aphrodite and Artemis are not. Aphrodite in the prologue says that she will inspire Phaedra with a fatal passion for the young Hippolytus because Hippolytus has failed to revere her power. Aphrodite says explicitly that she has no quarrel with Hippolytus for his devotion to Artemis, but she announces, " . . . his defiance of me will I avenge. . . . " Phaedra will die, but Aphrodite will get revenge, for in Phaedra's death Hippolytus will be destroyed.

Symbolically Aphrodite is the instinctive power of love, an elemental force with powers for good and for evil, beneficent to man only when duly recognized. It is a creative force without which human life is impossible, as the nurse explains to Phaedra:

> . . . *all things have their birth of her.*
> *'Tis she that sows love, gives increase thereof,*
> *Whereof all we that dwell on earth are sprung.*

Aphrodite is an unconquerable power of nature, a human instinct, neither moral nor immoral.[6] Phaedra appeals to Aphrodite as the force which makes for constancy in married life, while a hundred lines later the opportunistic old nurse, in an effort to save Phaedra's life, appeals to Aphrodite for aid in her infamous design to bring Phaedra and Hippolytus together.

Hippolytus represents a conflict between two extreme human attitudes, Aphrodite symbolizing passion and Artemis symbolizing chastity—complementary forces which must be reverenced. Deny either force utterly and there is disaster. Hippolytus, frequenter of woodland haunts, is a devotee of Artemis to the exclusion of Aphrodite. *Hippolytus* shows, therefore, not a conflict between good and evil, but a conflict between two partial goods.

When *Hippolytus* opens, Phaedra, essentially chaste, has struggled with her passion for her stepson Hippolytus but has been unable to gain control of herself. The conflict seems almost over. For three days she has fasted and now is resolved to die a silent death in preference to disgrace. In a few lines of restrained agony, before she has gained complete mastery of herself, her passionate nature, in need of sympathy, reveals the source of her struggle to the old nurse. But she herself does not pronounce the name of Hippolytus. That is left for the nurse—a fine dramatic touch.[7] The old nurse, in a lengthy argumentative passage of commonplaces, seeks to convince Phaedra that a married woman is not wrong in giving her love to another man. Failing in her effort, the nurse promises to allay Phaedra's passion by procuring from Hippolytus some token, an object or a word, to weave into a charm. Phaedra suspects that the nurse intends to speak to Hippolytus, but, exhausted with struggle and fasting, she does not attempt to deter her.

Here it might be noted that Euripides exhibits characters prone to act on their desires in spite of their better judgments. Such a character is Phaedra, who knows her error but is drawn irresistibly from her course:

> ... discretion dwells at least
> With many,—but we thus must look hereon:
> That which is good we learn and recognize,
> Yet practice not the lesson. ...

Hippolytus has sworn not to reveal the secret the nurse is about to tell him, but in a passing flash of indignation after he learns the nurse's dishonorable intent, he regrets his oath: "My tongue hath sworn: no oath is on my soul." After Hippolytus' angry denunciation of women, Phaedra finds it impossible to believe he will not reveal her desire to her husband; she then decides to write the letter which destroys Hippolytus but leaves her reputation clear. It is a tribute to the honesty of Hippolytus that when the time comes and he is denounced by Theseus for disloyalty, he offers a series of counterpleas but keeps his oath at the cost of his life.

Phaedra's suicide results from her inability to face Theseus' anticipated ire. In a choice between disgrace and death it is significant that she, like Sophocles' Jocasta, prefers to die. In Phaedra's death pity is invoked rather than disapprobation, in spite of her unjustified animosity toward Hippolytus. Although her hasty suicide prevents her from receiving the sympathy that Hippolytus and Theseus win, her reputation has been saved.[8]

Aphrodite, who foretold in the prologue that the unfortunate Phaedra would die as a pawn in her game of vengeance, foretold also the death of Hippolytus:

He knows not Hades' gates wide flung for him,
And this day's light the last his eyes shall see.

Hippolytus is a youth who loves to call his hounds and
race his horses and to worship Artemis with woven flowers
and converse in the woods. He is impetuous, but the servant
condones his impetuosity as characteristic of youth. When
Hippolytus defies Aphrodite, the servant asks the goddess
to forgive "If one that bears through youth a vehement
heart / Speak folly." But Aphrodite is not forgiving.

Later Theseus in his unthinking agony after the death of
his wife imputes to his son's youth the crime of incontinence:

Youths, I have proved,
Are no whit more than women continent,
When Cypris stirs a heart in flush of youth:
Yet all the strength of manhood helpeth them.

Hippolytus states his case succinctly to his father:

See'st thou yon sun
And earth?—within their compass is no man—
Though thou deny it—chaster-souled than I.

And though Aphrodite rebukes him for his conduct, Hippolytus has always been pious toward the gods and just in
his dealings with men.

For I have learnt, first, to revere the Gods,
Then, to have friends which seek to do no wrong, . . .

he reminds his father. His assertion the chorus of Troe-
zenian women believe, but not Theseus.

Hippolytus recognizes Phaedra's good intention in writing
the incriminating letter—an indication of his own nobility

of character. When provoked by his father's condemnation on account of the letter, he explains:

> *Her honour by dishonour did she guard:*
> *I, in a sore strait, cleave to honour still.*

Although Hippolytus does not recognize completely the irony of his situation, he feels that he has got no good from his chastity. He now knows that Phaedra valued honor more than desire. He knows also that he did right in resisting her. His explanation exonerates him in the eyes of the audience, though Theseus does not perceive his son's innocence until he is informed by Artemis, too late. Theseus, too, is a tragic victim.

Revealing the moral inconsistencies which he discovers in popular theology, Euripides has Artemis affirm:

> *The wicked, and withal*
> *Their children and their homes, do we destroy.*

But Theseus, like Hippolytus, does not suffer because he is wicked. Artemis in the end vindicates him because of error done in ignorance. Theseus suffers in spite of his goodness, although he errs, like so many tragic characters, as a result of hasty judgment. Frequently the innocent suffer in Euripides' plays, but Euripides, unlike Sophocles, makes no attempt to palliate such suffering.

The death of both Phaedra and Hippolytus must be viewed in the tragic framework that Aphrodite has made, but it is Artemis in the closing scene who completes the revelation of the inner tragedy. When the mangled Hippolytus is borne in, protesting his innocence, and when he bursts forth with the wish that men could but curse the gods as the gods curse men, Artemis can only assure him that her divinity will eventually avenge itself on the malignant power of Aphrodite, and promise him perpetual honors after his death. However, by explaining the entire plot to Theseus, just before Hippolytus is brought in, Artemis vindicates the reputation of both Hippolytus and Phaedra:

> *But I am come to show the righteousness*
> *Of thy son, that in fair fame he may die,*
> *And thy wife's fever-flame,—yet in some sort*
> *Her nobleness. She, stung by goads of her*
> *Whom we, who joy in purity, abhor*
> *Most of all Gods, was lovesick for thy son.*
> *Her reason fought her passion, and she died*
> *Through schemes wherein she had no part: her nurse*
> *Told under oath-seal to thy son her pangs:*
> *He, even as was righteous, would not heed*
> *The tempting; no, nor when sore-wronged of thee*
> *Broke he the oath's pledge, for he feared the Gods.*
> *But she, adread to be of sin convict,*
> *Wrote that false writing, and by treachery so*
> *Destroyed thy son:—and thou believedst her!*

The words of the chaste Artemis, who mitigates the fault of Theseus—

> *Not of thy will thou slewest him, and well*
> *May men transgress when Gods are thrusting on*

—echo the words of the gross old nurse to the unyielding but passionate Phaedra:[9]

> *Tush—if more good than evil is in thee,*
> *Who art but human, thou shalt do full well.*
> *Nay, darling, from thy deadly thought refrain,*
> *And from presumption—sheer presumption this,*
> *That one should wish to be more strong than Gods.*

The main impression left by *Hippolytus* is that of the pathos of human life at the mercy of capricious divinities. When Hippolytus protests his innocence and the injustice of his lot, "All vainly I reverenced God, and in vain unto man was I just," it is Artemis, defender of his innocence, who makes the ironic reply, "Thine own heart's nobleness hath ruined thee." Hippolytus has the virtue of piety— obedience to the will of Artemis; yet Hippolytus is destroyed. It will be remembered that obedience to the will of a vengeful Apollo was sufficient to save Aeschylus' Orestes because Aeschylus had an all pervading conception of divine justice.

Hippolytus suffers out of proportion to his offense, and the fruit of his suffering is his forgiveness of his erring father, who must live on in a state of tragic enlightenment. In the forgiveness of father by son Euripides has manipulated the action of the drama to suit his tragic idea and has expressed the pathos of the dying Hippolytus.

Romeo and Juliet

IN THE tragedy of *Romeo and Juliet*, as in *Hippolytus*, fate presides from the prologue over the destiny of the protagonists and ultimately brings about their death. In both tragedies disaster results from defiance of superhuman forces—of fate operating through the feud between the Montagues and Capulets and of the equally inexorable Aphrodite working her will through the passionate Phaedra. Unwisely ignoring obstacles in their course, Romeo and Juliet and Hippolytus attempt to shake off the inauspicious yoke of destiny. Nevertheless, it should be noted that their impetuous defiance redounds to their credit. In the case of Romeo and Juliet it is a mark of the intensity of their love; in the case of Hippolytus it is a measure of his chastity. It should be observed also that the emphasis is on the noble feeling rather than on the noble action of the protagonists, for in tragedies of pathos the hero has little opportunity to make important moral choices. The hero may be considered the maker of his own destiny only when his wrong choices arise from an inner fault.[10]

The prologue of *Romeo and Juliet* announces the operation of fate in the lives of two "star-cross'd" lovers, and the idea of fate is reiterated frequently in references to fortune and the "inauspicious stars," and in forebodings of trouble imminent, especially in dreams. Fate is in the background of the feud which is the obstacle to the lovers' open marriage; indeed, in the perspective of Romeo and Juliet fate is the feud. The "ancient grudge" breaks out in the opening scene, first among the domestics of the two households, then among members of both houses, and finally between old Montague and old Capulet themselves. Mercutio's death at the hands of Tybalt, and Tybalt's death at the hands of Romeo as avenger, result from the feud. After the death of Tybalt, Romeo's effort to disentangle himself from the web of circumstances in which his impetuosity has involved him is futile. Romeo is banished, and the course of his love is, as the prologue declares, "death-mark'd."

The youth of the two lovers contributes to the pathos of the tragedy. The immaturity of Romeo and Juliet is marked at the beginning, until love suddenly matures their outlook. Romeo at first imagines he loves Rosaline, but he later realizes it is infatuation at a distance, a mooning in the dark, a desire that can be expressed in superficial conceits. Likewise, Juliet at the beginning is a girl ready to place filial obedience above love, willing to respect her parents' wishes with regard to her marriage.

Romeo goes to the masque to prove his obdurate Rosaline fairest of women, and there by chance he meets Juliet and is entranced—a tribute to Juliet's beauty. Romeo, now in love, does not moon over the object of his affection, nor does he thereafter boast his ability to love. Later, Juliet, secretly married to Romeo, can no longer accept her parents' choice of Paris as husband, even though the worldly old Angelica, epitomizing the traditional stage nurse,[11] urges a policy of expediency, aware as she is of Juliet's marriage.

Romeo and Juliet is the tragedy of two young lovers frankly expressing their impatient affection in lyric beauty. Their love is made poignant by their isolation in a misunderstanding world; they move in a sphere where youthful passion has no place.

The tragic effect is enhanced by the warm quality of physical beauty embodied in Juliet and praised so frequently by Romeo. Romeo, banished after a few hours with his new-made wife, returns to find her supposedly dead in the tomb, and pays love and beauty a last tribute:

> *O my love! my wife!*
> *Death, that hath suck'd the honey of thy breath,*
> *Hath had no power yet upon thy beauty.*

But the greatest tragic effect demands for our sense of justice some degree of guilt on the hero's part. Romeo makes no blameworthy mistakes; his errors are the result of adverse circumstances. Fortune's fool he is indeed, as the Friar's letter miscarries and as he kills himself before Juliet awakes. Had he received the letter, had he been in-

formed of Juliet's sleep-inducing plan, there would have
been no tragedy of Romeo and Juliet.

Like Euripides' *Hippolytus*, the tragedy of *Romeo and
Juliet* represents the pathos of youth with unswerving devotion to an ideal, perishing through no fault of its own.
The death of the young lovers brings about a reconciliation
of members of the warring houses. The sins of the fathers
are forgiven, as Hippolytus forgave his erring father. And
as Artemis promised perpetual homage to Hippolytus after
his untimely destruction, so old Montague and old Capulet
will erect statues symbolic of the pathos of unmerited death.

FIVE

ROMANTIC IRONY

R OMANTIC irony" has been variously defined by Schlegel, Tieck,[1] and others, until the very concept
becomes amorphous. Sedgewick finds that "the romanti-
cists themselves juggle with irony until the word loses
meaning; they seem to vary the sense they put upon
it, according as their humours and conceits may govern."[2]
Chevalier aptly describes what he calls irony, and what I
have here called romantic irony: "In actual experience,
Irony characterizes the attitude of one who, when confronted with the choice of two things that are mutually
exclusive, chooses both. Which is but another way of saying
that he chooses neither."[3] In this book the doubtful issue
of action, or the resolution of a drama in ambiguity, is
called romantic irony.

Aeschylus and Sophocles seem to present in their tragedies an ethical outlook which is consistent. Although more
plays by Euripides are extant than by either of the other
two Greek tragedians (nineteen of his more than ninety),
critics find it hard to agree about the interpretation of many
of Euripides' plays. Thompson calls his *Bacchae* "ethically
the most ambiguous of all Greek plays."[4]

Aristotelian *ethos* depends upon choice and, at its best,
results from a character's making good choices. When
standards of conduct are subjective, hence fluctuating, as
they are in romantic irony, a choice can be called neither

good nor bad, and a character cannot be held responsible for his actions. A spectator finds difficulty in identifying himself through "pity and fear" with a sufferer whose nature is dubious, for to arouse those emotions the character must be primarily "good." With whom should one identify oneself in the *Bacchae,* or with whom in *Antony and Cleopatra?* Aristotle's doctrine of *ethos* does not embrace the romantic point of view.

The Bacchae and Antony and Cleopatra

The Bacchae

BETWEEN Euripides' *Hippolytus* and his *Bacchae* similarities have more than once been discovered.[5] Perhaps the most palpable likeness appears in the conflict between two opposed and complementary forces, between Aphrodite and Artemis in *Hippolytus* and between Dionysus and Pentheus in the *Bacchae;* but so far as the resolution of the tragedies is concerned, the differences seem of salient importance.

In *Hippolytus* the struggle so far as the leading characters are concerned is resolved by superhuman agents; Phaedra is merely an instrument in the hands of Aphrodite to bring about the destruction of Hippolytus. Hippolytus succumbs to the divine power of Aphrodite with little struggle. At the close of the tragedy there is little doubt about the author's attitude toward his human characters. Hippolytus dies protesting his innocence, and his reputation is vindicated by the divine and opposing power of Artemis. That Hippolytus is one-sided is true, worshiping chastity, as he does, too vehemently; but that he should yield to Phaedra and thus to the power of Aphrodite in her aspect of un-chastity is nowhere implied, for his honor is finally upheld by Artemis. The faultless Hippolytus is in the end over-come by a divine power too great for him to withstand.

In the *Bacchae* the interest in the struggle centers not on the divine but on the human level, between the mortal Pentheus and the god Dionysus disguised as one of his own votaries. The fact that the god appears personally to con-front the Theban king who scorns his worship, complicates the plot[6]—although it is not so much the fact that he ap-pears in mortal form as that he appears ambiguously.

Frequently it is not difficult to determine with what char-acter in the tragedy the sympathy of the audience should lie and who, therefore, is the tragic hero; but in the *Bacchae* our sympathy seems to be invoked for Dionysus in the first part, for Pentheus in the second part. Dionysus, purporting to dispense justice, assumes the dual role of benevolent and vindictive deity, and one is therefore compelled to conclude that if Dionysus is the hero, Pentheus is the villain and the tragedy is a plain statement of poetic justice. If Pentheus is the hero, then he falls before a superior force, not a superior justice. Has the god been unjust to the mortal or the mortal unjust to the god? Who is the oppressor and who the oppressed?[7] In this ambiguity lies the problem of the *Bacchae*.

Pentheus at the beginning of the tragedy is prejudiced and headstrong[8] in his effort to suppress Dionysus and his worship in Thebes. Dionysus, in the beginning a benevo-lent god, has come to his native Thebes from Asia to assert his godhead—his divine birth as son of Zeus and Semele,[9] to vindicate his mother's good name against kinsman calum-niators, and to establish his worship in Thebes. Because

Pentheus denies his godhead and opposes his worship, asserting that the legend of Semele is a pious fraud invented
by Cadmus to save his daughter's reputation, Dionysus has
driven Agave, the mother of Pentheus, her sisters, and
other Theban women to the hills to join the bacchanalian
revels. Pentheus insists that the Bacchic madness is a pretext for licentiousness. He suspects that the god masks
Aphrodite and that his votaries, driven by lust and intoxi-
cated by wine, follow a foreign impostor intent upon propa-
gating an immoral religion.

In defense of Dionysus, it should be observed that the
god does not at this time intend to use force to uphold his
worship. He announces in the prologue:

> *If Thebes in wrath*
> *Take arms to chase her Bacchants from the hills,*
> *Leading my Maenads I will clash in fight.*

Furthermore, in support of the deity, the chorus of Bac-
chanals, who have followed him from Asia, sing with an
air of rapture a warning to the irreverent:

> *O happy to whom is the blessedness given*
> *To be taught in the Mysteries sent from heaven,*
> *Who is pure in his life, through whose soul the unsleeping*
> *Revel goes sweeping!*

Cadmus acknowledges the god: "Not I contemn the Gods,
I, mortal-born!" Although Cadmus' recognition is largely a
matter of expediency, he warns his grandson to whom he
has given the throne:

> *For, though this God were no God,—as thou sayest,—*
> *God be he called of thee: in glorious fraud*
> *Be Semele famed as mother of a God:*
> *So upon all our house shall honour rest.*

Teiresias acknowledges the god as a matter of conviction; he is a proponent of the doctrine that faith needs no support in reason. " 'Tis not for us to reason touching Gods." Teiresias links Demeter, giver of food, with Dionysus, giver of wine, as the greatest of man's benefactors. In the gift of wine he has granted to mortals release from toil and care in sleep, and to the gods he has given a libation. To Pentheus' charge of impurity Teiresias answers:

> Dionysus upon women will not thrust
> Chastity: in true womanhood inborn
> Dwells temperance touching all things evermore.
> This must thou heed; for in his Bacchic rites
> The virtuous-hearted shall not be undone.

Thus the purity of the religion is affirmed not only by Teiresias, by the chorus, and by the testimonies of the herdsman and the messenger, but by the statement of Dionysus himself: "His rites loathe him that worketh godlessness." No evidence is presented to the contrary.

Nevertheless, although the beauty and ecstasy of the Dionysiac worship is often acclaimed, it is not without its unseemly aspects.[10] Teiresias and Cadmus, old men dancing in fawn skins with ivy-wreathed heads, the only willing votaries, appear ridiculous not only to the prejudiced Pentheus but even to themselves. Teiresias says to his companion, as the two go forth to worship:

> Come with me, ivy-wand in hand,
> Essay to upbear my frame, as I do thine.
> Shame if two greybeards fell! . . .

Their piety is worthy of respect, but what of their practice? As part of the pure, enthusiastic worship, the chorus as frankly admits the bloody and savage side—the rending of wild beasts as well as the miraculous flow of milk and honey. The outlandish aspect of the religion is further emphasized by the herdsman's account of the bacchanalian rending of cattle and the plunder of two armed villages, overcome by the sacred thyrsi.

Dionysus in his dual role of beneficent and vindictive deity is indeed a powerful god—even as Teiresias warns Pentheus. Nevertheless, the headstrong Pentheus has already imprisoned as many of the followers of Dionysus as he could apprehend, and he now gives orders to imprison the "girl-faced stranger," who is presently brought in by an apologetic servant. The servant reports the miraculous escape of the imprisoned Bacchae. In a long passage of *stichomythia* Dionysus and Pentheus confront each other. Pentheus threatens to punish the god for refusing to divulge the Bacchic mysteries, even to the uninitiated! He is threatened in turn with divine punishment for folly and impiety. Climaxing his *hybristic* conduct, Pentheus clips the god's hair and wrests the symbolic thyrsus from his hand.[11] The outraged deity threatens nemesis for Pentheus' *hybris:*[12]

> *On thee Dionysus shall requite*
> *These insults—he whose being thou hast denied.*

Dionysus is imprisoned in a stable.

However, nemesis is not long delayed. Dionysus, issuing presently from his imprisonment, reports the approaching madness of Pentheus, who has bound a bull in the stall, thinking it his prisoner, and who, supposing his prisoner has escaped from the burning stable, has attacked a wraith in his delusion. Pentheus is slowly being maddened by the rejected god, so that at length he is content to take as guide the deity he had earlier sought to destroy.

Dressed in woman's garments, effeminately anxious about his appearance, Pentheus emerges with his companion, whom he mistakes for a bull, to spy upon his enemies. With thyrsus in hand, he is as ridiculous as were Teiresias and Cadmus in fawn skins. Pentheus goes forth to die at his mother's hands, thus fulfilling the prophecy of Dionysus:

> *And he shall know Zeus' son*
> *Dionysus, who hath risen at last a God*
> *Most terrible, yet kindest unto men.*

Thus far Dionysus has been acting in self-defense.

The terrible aspect of Dionysus appears just before Pentheus' death. During the encounter with the Bacchae, Pentheus is released from his madness, most cruelly to realize his horrible destruction and to recognize at last the godhead of Dionysus. To his mother he cries for mercy, while she, thinking she rends a lion's whelp, is first to tear him limb from limb—"Happy Agave!" The ecstatic Agave, carrying her son's head home, receives the acclaim of the chorus—sympathetic throughout to Dionysus, the avenger of the unrighteous. When Cadmus enters, carrying on a bier the remains of Pentheus' corpse, madness gradually leaves Agave and she realizes the horrors she has committed. Then follows the lament for Pentheus, sole heir and protector of Cadmus and the house of Thebes.[13] The sympathy of the audience, heretofore with the despised god, is shifted at length to Pentheus, the demented mortal overcome by a ruthless deity.

In the end the entire family of Cadmus suffers punishment. No member of the ancient house is left in his native Thebes. The chorus holds that Pentheus' death was justified, but it cannot but admit that Cadmus' punishment is heavy.[14] Agave acknowledges guilt, but charges that the god's vengeance has been excessive. To her accusation, "It fits not that in wrath Gods be as men," Dionysus can only reply that thus it has long been ordained—an unsatisfactory answer for a deity.

Both Pentheus and Hippolytus are overthrown by an outraged deity, at the hands of parents acting in ignorance. Hippolytus is proclaimed innocent by an opposing deity; Pentheus, although not innocent, has suffered beyond his deserts. However, Pentheus is too nearly the villain in the first part of the tragedy to deserve complete sympathy. And although Dionysus has suffered the abuse of Pentheus, Dionysus is too relentless in the second part of the tragedy to win wholehearted approval. In the ambivalence of sympathy for the tragic hero, whether Pentheus or Dionysus, lies the romantic irony of the *Bacchae*.

Antony and Cleopatra

ROMANTIC irony inheres in the ambiguous resolution of both the *Bacchae* and *Antony and Cleopatra*. The irony arises, in part, from the author's lack of assertion of a well-defined attitude toward his characters. Thus, in the *Bacchae* Euripides does not condemn Dionysus for bringing to fulfillment the ungodlike "works of the Gods." And Shakespeare neither glorifies nor condemns the illicit love of his protagonists. Adultery is not, as in *Hippolytus*, evil. Antony and Cleopatra are a law unto themselves. Antony declares

> *... the nobleness of life*
> *Is to do thus, when such a mutual pair*
> *And such a twain can do't ...*

and invites the world to know of their "peerless" position.

In part, the irony arises from an ambiguity of interpretation of one of the leading characters in each play, of Dionysus in the *Bacchae* and of Cleopatra in *Antony and Cleopatra,* and the ultimate undoing of the unambiguous character by his ambiguous opposite. Cleopatra is an enchanter, an Oriental enchanter, like the Eastern "impostor" Dionysus, and Antony is aware that he is losing himself in infatuation for her. Antony, oblivious to the call of Rome, is compensating for his strenuous action following the fall of Julius Caesar until the time of his victories at Philippi, by a life of ease:

> *Let Rome in Tiber melt, and the wide arch*
> *Of the rang'd empire fall! Here is my space.*
> *Kingdoms are clay; our dungy earth alike*
> *Feeds beast as man....*

If one supposes that Antony is the hero of *Antony and Cleopatra* and likens him to Pentheus, a possible hero of the *Bacchae,* one finds in each case a man caught between two powerful forces, between the extremes of emotion on the one hand and reason on the other—and unable to pursue a safe course between them. Antony follows the perilous course too close to the passion of Cleopatra, while Pentheus follows the equally disastrous course too remote from the worship of Dionysus. In deviation from the middle path destruction lies.

Antony's destruction is implicit in the opening lines, when his friend observes, " ... this dotage of our general's / O'erflows the measure." And Antony, unlike Pentheus, recognizes his own danger. Although he exults without shame in his devotion to Cleopatra, he remembers momentarily his dead wife Fulvia and his duty to Rome[15] when he says, "I must from this enchanting queen break off; ... " but before he leaves Egypt it is apparent that, captivated by her "cunning past man's thought," he will soon return to this "serpent of old Nile."

> ... I go from hence
> Thy soldier, servant; making peace or war
> As thou [affect'st].

The first act is largely concerned with the private affairs of Antony and Cleopatra, while the second act is concerned with the public fortune. In an effort to cement a breach with Octavius Caesar, since Pompey threatens both, Antony temporarily takes in marriage the young ruler's sister Octavia, "whose virtue and whose general graces speak." The marriage is one of expediency, for Antony perceives that " ... though I make this marriage for my peace, / I' th' East my pleasure lies."

Enobarbus too knows that Antony will not long remain away from the lure of Cleopatra, and in a rhapsody of words he praises her ambiguously:

> Age cannot wither her, nor custom stale
> Her infinite variety. Other women cloy
> The appetites they feed, but she makes hungry
> Where most she satisfies; ...

and it should be remembered that Enobarbus is Shakespeare's tragic chorus.[16] However much Shakespeare might have taken from Plutarch for the interpretation of Antony and Cleopatra, Enobarbus is the one character who is almost wholly Shakespeare's own, a cynical, soft-hearted Enobarbus who deserts and dies in disillusionment.

In the third act the public and the private fortunes are joined, in the themes of war and love. Cleopatra has "nodded him to her" and Antony begins kissing away kingdoms to Cleopatra and the "unlawful issue" of their "lust." In defense of Rome's interest in the Mediterranean world, Octavius Caesar prepares to fight Antony at Actium. Cleopatra makes the crucial error of entering the conflict. Refusing the advice of Enobarbus, she "will not stay behind." During the course of the naval battle she flees, and Antony insures his defeat by following her. Against his better judgment, Enobarbus pursues for a while longer the "wounded chance" of his chief, remembering in the graying general the spirit the soothsayer discovered:

> *Noble, courageous, high, unmatchable,*
> *Where Caesar's is not. . . .*

Nevertheless, the "triple pillar" of whom Pompey could say, "His soldiership / Is twice the other twain, . . . " now realizes that he holds a "sword, made weak by my affection," and that Cleopatra, more powerful than Caesar, is his conqueror.

To Cleopatra's question, "Is Antony or we in fault for this?" Enobarbus must answer, excusing Cleopatra's flight: "Antony only, that would make his will/Lord of his reason."

As Pentheus fell under the hypnotic power of Dionysus, so Antony is yielding gradually to the deceptive influence of Cleopatra. But Antony, unike Pentheus, is aware of a danger in Cleopatra's power and has moments of mental recoil, even though his fortunes are by this time so inextricably entwined with Cleopatra's in Egypt that he finds it impossible to return to his Roman interests. Jealousy, when Caesar's messenger ceremoniously kisses Cleopatra's hand, prompts Antony's recollection of the legitimate claims of Octavia:[17]

Have I my pillow left unpress'd in Rome,
Forborne the getting of a lawful race,
And by a gem of women, to be abus'd
By one that looks on feeders?

He accuses himself of having followed blindly a wrong course:

And when we in our viciousness grow hard—
O misery on't!—the wise gods seel our eyes;
In our own filth drop our clear judgements; make us
Adore our errors; laugh at 's while we strut
To our confusion.

Of Caesar's military exploits the older and heretofore victorious Antony has occasion now to be jealous:

He makes me angry with him; for he seems
Proud and disdainful, harping on what I am,
Not what he knew I was.

Antony's anger makes him fearless, as Enobarbus observes, and he resolves to go forth gallantly, after Cleopatra has buckled on his armor. A brief victory on land is followed by a final defeat at sea when his fleet deserts to Caesar. Overcome by his loss, Antony hastily concludes, "This foul Egyptian hath betrayed me."

Cleopatra's ruse to win Antony to her by report of her death then results in the death of Antony.[18] In some respects Antony's death resembles that of Brutus, although Brutus by his stoical fortitude "only overcame himself" in a way that Antony does not. One of Antony's motives, like one of Brutus' motives, is to rob the enemy of the boast of slaying him, and he advises his friend Eros to strike: "Thou strik'st not me, 'tis Caesar thou defeat'st." Eros, to avoid killing his master, turns the sword upon himself, and in the suicide of Eros Antony finds a noble example of one who seems to bear death "lightly." Thus prompted, in part by the desire to escape the ignominy of Caesar's triumphal procession, but more significantly to be a "bridegroom" in a death which will reunite him with Cleopatra, he falls upon his sword amorously—only to learn shortly afterward that his bride has not preceded him in death. Nevertheless, the thoughts of the dying Antony, hoisted up to Cleopatra locked in her monument, though partly concerned with the restoration of his reputation, redeemed by a "Roman" death, are more concerned with the safety of Cleopatra, as he urges her to seek refuge at the hands of Caesar.

For Cleopatra the world is empty without Antony:[19] "Young boys and girls / Are level now with men"; and, humbled, she cries:

> No more but [e'en] a woman, and commanded
> By such poor passion as the maid that milks
> And does the meanest chares.

Later she can say, "My desolation does begin to make / A better life." She, like Antony, partly to avoid a life in Rome "eternal" in Caesar's triumph, resolves to die

> . . . after the high Roman fashion,
> And make Death proud to take us.

But more significantly, with a maid trimming up her diadem, she satisfies her "immortal longings" by hastening "again for Cydnus" to meet Mark Antony before Iras, who is dying of grief for her mistress' adversity, meets the "curled Antony" and receives the kiss it is her "heaven to have." She anticipates the bite of the asp but " . . . as a

lover's pinch, / Which hurts, and is desir'd." At last Cleopatra, who in her duplicity had "such celerity in dying"—
she whom Enobarbus had seen "die twenty times"—is
"marble-constant" in her resolve. She considers herself
worthy the name of wife of a Roman husband:[20]

> *Husband, I come!*
> *Now to that name my courage prove my title!*

Re-echoing the high Roman note, the austere Caesar,
though deprived of his triumphal glory, gives command
for a common grave and pronounces a final eulogy:

> *High events as these*
> *Strike those that make them; and their story is*
> *No less in pity than his glory which*
> *Brought them to be lamented.*

Caesar, in according pity to Antony, cannot refrain from
boasting of "his glory," even though his own triumph is
diminished by Antony's death.

So far as the public fortune is concerned, the tragedy
closes with the death of Antony and the chapter the Ides
of March had begun. Caesar fittingly proclaims:

> *The death of Antony*
> *Is not a single doom; in the name lay*
> *A moiety of the world.*

But so far as Shakespeare is concerned, the tragedy closes
with the death of the lovers,[21] and Shakespeare, unlike
Plutarch and Dryden, discovers no moral in the lovers'
tragedy.[22] In a world in which the forces of right and
wrong are neutral, Cleopatra, like Dionysus, is a principle
which, though it destroys, is yet exalted in the ambiguity
of romantic irony.

SIX

STOICISM

THE STOICS were many and their doctrines various, but there are a few general principles which seem to pervade their philosophy. Stoicism, springing from the teachings of Socrates and transmitted through Plato and Aristotle, emphasized the supremacy of reason leading to right action. Error in action might lead to suffering. Suffering (as in the tragedies of Aeschylus and Sophocles, contemporaries of Socrates) was a school for character. Wisdom came from suffering.

But Stoicism went off on a tangent from Socratic teaching. The Stoic tended to emphasize the importance of reason leading to right *motive;* he stressed the significance of the will rather than the act. Thus, *ethos* centers in the right intention of the hero, in his will to achieve virtue at any cost, at the cost of loyalty to family, to the state, or even at the cost of life itself.

Aeschylus and Sophocles could not conceive of a moral being outside the city-state, or *polis.* Their characters live in a social order, no matter how bad it may be. The Stoic, although generally loyal to the state, could renounce even that allegiance if it conflicted with the attainment of his ideal. Hence, the Stoic might be forced to suffer for what the world calls evil action, but is not by him called evil because it is dictated by his nobility of purpose.[1] Seneca had difficulty being loyal under the intolerable political conditions of Nero's empire and so sought refuge in the philosophy of Stoicism, which he hoped would make him immune to the suffering into which his commendable motives might lead him—immune even to the fear of death.

Stoicism has little in common with Aristotle's conception of *ethos*, for the ideal stoic hero, adhering to his own right intentions, would have no fault, and hence would arouse no fear; nor would he arouse pity, since attainment of fortitude would make him immune to what the rest of the world called suffering.

Seneca's *Hercules Oetaeus* presents the conception of a stoic hero, Hercules, comparable to Brutus in Shakespeare's *Julius Caesar*. Hercules and Brutus are men in whom stoical strength of purpose leads to a death over which they triumph by perfection of fortitude.

Hercules Oetaeus and *Julius Caesar*

Hercules Oetaeus

ALTHOUGH Greek tragedy always recognized powers beyond the control of man, it emphasized a certain degree of freedom on the part of man. Aeschylean and Sophoclean tragedy find such good as man may hope to achieve less in the operation of external forces than in man's own activity. The Greeks, in their search to discover what constitutes human excellence, held that it is imperative for every man to struggle until he attains such excellence, or *arete*.[2]

Aeschylus is the first great exponent in tragedy of the truism that wisdom, the essence of noble character, comes to man through suffering. But Sophocles stressed even more than Aeschylus the importance of *arete*. Although disaster in man's struggle appears in Sophocles generally as a result of the violation of a moral law, man is revealed, either on account of ignorance or in allegiance to still higher obligation, as only partially guilty and is in the end, like Oedipus at Colonus, vindicated.

In Euripides' dramas which best reveal ethical action it is apparent that emphasis has shifted from an assertion of man's strength in resisting adversity to a manifestation of his weakness in facing external forces. Euripides' conclusion is that it is seldom possible for man to achieve *arete* because the odds are too great against him. Man's life is at the mercy of whatever forces control the universe. In both Euripides' and Seneca's plays human beings suffer as a result of supernatural caprice; retribution therefore has little relation to the moral deserts of the sufferer. However, only on the hypothesis of freedom to achieve *arete* can one speak of moral guilt and therefore of virtue and vice, a dichotomy underlying the concept of *arete*.

The attainment of *arete*, which came to mean for the Stoic a kind of excellence called virtue, is the chief concern of stoic ethics, as represented in the writings of Seneca and elsewhere. To live "according to nature" is the phrase which expresses the stoic ethical ideal.[3] By surrendering his will to nature, which appears fundamentally rational and good, the Stoic sought to achieve virtue and thereby whatever happiness is humanly possible. Such a surrender involved a discipline in adversity, guided by right reason based upon knowledge of stoic philosophy. The Stoic sought to discipline his inner life in conformity with what his reason told him was nature's intention. Though he could change nature but little, he could change himself.[4]

In such a training the will, or the motive, was considered

more important than the deed,[5] and the good will was believed to be attainable except in cases of insanity when irrationality gives a false conception of what is good.[6] The perfection of such a discipline was a virtue immune to misfortune.

It is probably not surprising then that Seneca found his most congenial source in the dramas of Euripides, "most tragic of the poets." To Euripides' unhappy endings culminating frequently in pathos felt for the vanquished sufferer, Seneca added an escape from a hostile world to a triumph in stoic philosophy. Hercules in *Hercules Oetaeus* is the outstanding embodiment of stoic philosophy in Senecan tragedy—of the principle that adversity is given to man as an occasion to display virtue. In *Hercules Oetaeus* the hero wins immortality through valiant endurance of suffering.[7]

Hercules is a strong man, and his strength, more than mortal, he has frequently used in the service of mankind. He has overcome the world and has established peace throughout the earth. He has conquered Pluto's region beneath the earth and all lands have praised his deeds. This Hercules proclaims in the prologue, concluding with the mention of his latest exploit, the overthrow of the king of Oechalia. But the latest exploit Deianira, wife of Hercules, cannot forget, for Hercules has destroyed Oechalia and her king for the purpose of taking captive the king's daughter, Iole. Jealousy on the part of Deianira, leading to the heroic death of Hercules, is the theme of *Hercules Oetaeus*.

Deianira is bitterly jealous of the beautiful young captive, whom Hercules loves even more now that she has lost her father's house and her personal adornments. Deianira complains, " . . . out of pity, perchance, he loves her very woes. . . . " The nurse tries to comfort Deianira, but Deianira cannot put aside the thought, "Whate'er in me was sought in former days has vanished or is failing along with me. Old age with hastening steps hath taken much, and much of it hath motherhood stolen from me."

Deianira, proud of her position as daughter-in-law of Jove and wife of Hercules, scornfully declares her husband a trifler in love, a philanderer, and a destroyer of men— one who has deceived the world into thinking that Juno is "answerable for his crimes." Madly she concludes: "He whom thou seest going, big with fame, from town to town, wearing the spoil of a tawny lion on his back; who gives kingdoms to the lowly and takes them from the proud, his dread hand laden with a massive club; whose triumphs the far off Seres sing, and whoe'er besides dwells in the whole known world,—he is a trifler, nor does the charm of glory urge him on. He goes wandering o'er the earth, not in the hope that he may rival Jove, nor that he may fare illustrious through Grecian cities. Some one to love he seeks; his quest is maidens' chambers. If any is refused him, she is ravished; against nations doth he rage, midst ruins seeks his brides, and unrestrained excess is called heroic."

Deianira recognizes she is doing wrong in planning vengeance upon Hercules, but she at first excuses herself on account of her passion: "That I am doing a fearful crime, e'en I myself confess; but passion bids me do it." As she later declares, she loves her husband, but she shrinks from the humiliation of being supplanted in his affections. She is willing to risk death for revenge. Vehemently she cries, "Ah, sweet, 'tis sweet to go to the shades as bride of Hercules,—but not without my vengeance. If Iole from my Hercules has conceived a child, with mine own hands will I tear it forth untimely, and by her very wedding torches' glare will I face the harlot. Let him in wrath slay me as victim on his nuptial day, so I but fall on the corpse of Iole. Happy he lies who crushes those he hates."

The suggestion of the nurse that Deianira try to recover her husband's love by recourse to magic, reminds Deianira of the blood Nessus presented her in his hoof. This poisonous charm the dying centaur gave with the promise that his blood smeared on a garment as gift to an unfaithful husband would restore love. Deianira sends the fatal gift.

When Hercules' son Hyllus rushes in and describes to his mother his father's agonizing suffering before death, as a result of putting on the robe, the repentant Deianira resolves upon instant self-destruction. Hyllus and the nurse try to dissuade her by nullifying her responsibility. "He does no sin who sins without intent," Hyllus pleads, and again, "Life has been granted many whose guilt lay in wrong judgment, not in act." Hyllus reminds his mother that Hercules in a fit of madness slew his former wife Megara and his two sons and "still, though thrice murderer, he forgave himself, but not his madness," and then "washed away his guilt and cleansed his hands." The intention was good, therefore the deed is to be forgiven, even as Hippolytus forgave his father, who meant well, in Euripides' *Hippolytus*.

Deianira's remorse at the loss of Hercules makes life a matter of indifference to her. Suicide will be a final act of renunciation; it will be also an avenue to pardon.[8] Deianira cries, "O my unconquered husband, my soul is innocent, though my hands have sinned." She realizes that "sometimes death is a punishment, but often 'tis a boon, and to many a way of pardon has it proved." She anticipates absolution at the hands of the gods of the lower world. Like Euripides' Phaedra, she proves herself innocent by self-inflicted death. She commits suicide in the madness of remorse, exculpating herself: " . . . mine was the crime of love." Later she will be exonerated when, after Hyllus' explanation, Hercules realizes her innocence. Her voluntary death, however, keeps her from receiving the sympathy which Hercules will later win by his stoical fortitude.

When Hercules discovers that he is dying, his first regret is that he who has slain so many monsters and men is now overcome ingloriously "by a woman's hand"—not by the hand of Juno, not even by that of an Amazon. In his raving effort to find the pest that is burning through his vitals he rips away his garment-gift and lays bare the flesh. As his anguish abates, his tears begin; but, like Sophocles' Oedipus, he is ashamed to weep, and "oft does his fortitude drain back his tears."

Only after Hercules has been told by Hyllus that the robe was dipped in the centaur's gore does Hercules become reconciled to his lot. Exclaiming, " . . . my fate unfolds itself," he remembers the oracular prophecy of his death and ceases to complain. He takes thought of the manner of his death—"Now let me choose a death glorious, renowned, illustrious, full worthy of myself"—and he attempts to console his mother Alcmena.

Philoctetes, who was commanded by Hercules to apply the torch to the funeral pyre on Mount Oeta, later reports his stoical death. As he lay down upon the pyre—"What victor ever stood in his chariot so joyfully triumphant? What tyrant king with such a countenance ever gave laws to nations? How calmly he bore his fate! Even our tears were stayed, grief's shock subsided, none grieves that he must perish. Now were we 'shamed to weep; Alcmena, herself, whose sex impels to mourning, stood with dry cheeks, a mother well-nigh equal to her son." Philoctetes tells of Hercules' triumph over bodily torment: "Thou wouldst suppose that Caucasus or Pindus or Athos was ablaze; no sound burst forth, save that the fire seemed groaning."

Later Alcmena appears carrying a funeral urn containing the ashes of Hercules, and lamenting, "O Sun, how great a mass has passed away to nothingness!" And yet she proudly cries, "What sepulchre, O son, what tomb is great enough for thee? Thy tomb is the whole wide world, and fame shall be thine epitaph."

He who had aspired to the stars as reward for his labors on earth has by his father Jove been granted his wish, and the deified Hercules speaks from the heavens: "... now has my valour borne me to the stars and to the gods themselves." The chorus in a few words pronounces a final judgment upon Hercules, the benefactor of mankind: "The brave live on...."

Hercules is not a Sophoclean type of hero who recognizes that he has done wrong and that his wrongdoing has contributed to his ruin. There is no suggestion that Seneca's Hercules has any tragic fault. Aristotle perceives that our deepest sympathy is elicited only when the tragic hero is lifelike, and thus implies a degree of weakness on the hero's part. Hercules makes no mistake; he feels no guilt. Deianira is merely the agent of fate bringing about the downfall of a faultless hero. Hercules' infidelity does not score against his character; it is merely the human motivation for Deia-

nira's jealousy. Hercules in his death becomes even more
stoically heroic than Hercules in his life, for in dying he
has greater opportunity to display his invincible fortitude.

In his *De Providentia* Seneca expounds his views on renunciation to the effect, as Greene explains, that "God protects the good man from moral evils, but allows him
hardships, thus giving him every good, including the good
fortune not to need good fortune."[9] And so man's development ends in a paradox: at the moment when his claim
to freedom is strongest, he realizes he is completely unfree,
a slave to fate—like Hercules, the heroic champion of the
stoic ideal.[10]

Seneca himself was inconsistent enough to acquire in-
fluential and lucrative positions in Rome as tutor and later
as minister under the young Nero when Nero's immaturity
allowed his advisers to be virtually emperor. He justified
his action by his readiness to give up his post when fate,
in the person of a jealous Nero, gave the command.

Seneca's constant battle with debility and disease led him
to contemplate suicide, a course from which he was once
deterred by consideration of his father's wishes, as Hercules
in *Hercules Furens* is saved by his father Amphitryon. Late
in life he yielded to the idea and committed suicide at the
instigation of the Emperor Nero, who suspected him of
aiding in a conspiracy.

Stoics such as Seneca held that since wealth, health, even
life itself are matters of indifference, suicide is sometimes
justified. Seneca's arguments for suicide result from a deep
perception of insecurity which existed side by side with
philosophic complacency. Indeed, the argument for suicide
reached its height in the writings of Seneca, under the intolerable conditions of Roman despotism.

STOICISM

It was difficult for a man of the highest social class to be virtuous in the reign of Nero, and the flawless perfection of a man of absolute reason was an impossible aspiration for the average Roman citizen. Since few men could attain the earthly satisfaction of reasoned virtue, the vision of perfection receded to an infinite distance. The Stoic asked what reward would compensate for his great renunciation. Assurance of immortality was too nebulous. Christianity at length gave consolation to the masses in the promise of rewards in a hereafter based upon merits on earth. Many of the stoic principles were in time incorporated in the doctrines of Christianity, the founder of which was a contemporary of Seneca.

Julius Caesar

STOICISM is an important element in the ethical conception underlying *Julius Caesar*. As Seneca's Hercules in *Hercules Oetaeus* is the Roman model of Stoicism, so Brutus in *Julius Caesar* aspires to important tenets of the stoic philosophy handed down through Plutarch.

Brutus is endowed by nature with qualities which compose the virtuous man, and these he has disciplined by reason in both public and private life. Hence his reason for the assassination of Caesar is more important to the tragedy of Brutus than the deed, for in joining the conspirators Brutus acts with the best intentions. Brutus admires Caesar. With Caesar as a man Brutus has no quarrel, nor are Caesar's previous misdeeds advanced as justification for the conspiracy. That Brutus loves Caesar is evident in the assassination scene. When Brutus stoops as petitioner and speaks, his words carry more than treacherous intent: "I kiss thy hand, but not in flattery, Caesar...." And

111

Caesar's astonished cry when he recognizes Brutus—"*Et tu Brute!*"—indicates Caesar's own high regard for his betrayer. Brutus argues:

> *I know no personal cause to spurn at him*
> *But for the general.*

By a process of rationalization he concludes that Caesar's acquisition of the crown would alter Caesar from the benevolent despot he is to a relentless tyrant. If Brutus could destroy Caesar's influence without destroying Caesar, he would do that:

> *O, that we then could come by Caesar's spirit,*
> *And not dismember Caesar!*

Shaping his course according to what he has rationalized as an honorable intent, Brutus joins the conspiracy because he conceives of the conspirators as acting in the cause of disinterested justice, as "purgers, not murderers."

Urged at first by Cassius, whose motive is mixed with envy, Brutus is led to perform unwillingly what he considers a duty. But Brutus is loyal to a mistaken sense of duty. He does not recognize that the days of the republic are over, nor that the unstable plebeians, so easily persuaded in the first scene, the artisans who once could profess loyalty to Pompey and now can pay homage to Caesar, are the fickle populace, unused to reason, who will first applaud his argumentative oration after Caesar's death and later transfer their loyalties after the appeal of Antony.

Brutus suffers from the consequences of actions which cannot be called evil because they are dictated by his nobility. Having concluded, from doubtful premises, that Caesar crowned would be Caesar tyrannical, hence having inferred the justice of his cause, Brutus is confident he can persuade the rabble to his viewpoint. But the ironic contrast between the deed and its consequences is first apparent when, after the scholarly Brutus has appealed to the crowd ("... censure me in your wisdom, and awake your senses, that you may the better judge"), the citizens, now most favorable to Brutus, call out, "Let him be Caesar," and "Caesar's better parts / Shall be crown'd in Brutus." Brutus had hoped that "ambition's debt" was paid, and that Rome would return to the republicanism which, as Cassius reminded him, his illustrious ancestor by the same name had promulgated.

The only serious charge brought against Caesar in the play is his ambition. That Caesar is not, in fact, without ambition is recognized, for the Caesar who thrice refused the coronet is later persuaded, by the treacherous Decius, with promise of a crown, to come forth, in spite of ill omens, to the senate house. But Caesar's ambition is in part admirable, like Oedipus', in that it subserves the state. Urged at the crucial moment to read the warning against the conspiracy, Caesar, attentive to public service, answers: "What touches us ourself shall be last serv'd." Stepping into the intrigue of the conspirators, he wins the audience's sympathy just as does Agamemnon enmeshed in the net of his murderers. Antony's display of Caesar's hole-filled mantle, like Orestes' display of the robe in which Agamemnon was slain, wins further sympathy in the course of Antony's oration exonerating Caesar of a venial fault. But even though Caesar dead, as Caesar living, dominates the action of the tragedy, and the vengeful spirit of Caesar, of which Antony and Octavius are the agents, vanquishes Brutus at Philippi, the interest focuses on Brutus' character.

Seneca's Hercules made no mistake; he felt no guilt. Brutus in his awareness of his noble intentions never acknowledges error and hence feels no guilt. From the time when he is led by Cassius into conduct to which he is averse and which his esteem for Caesar resists, from the time he resolves to join the conspiracy, he does not waver in his purpose but persists in what he considers a duty. Brutus is a protagonist who falls on account of his futile opposition to the spirit of the titular hero, Caesar. His action is dictated by his aspiration to a humanly unattainable ideal of the state. Brutus' tragedy lies in the contrast between his admirable motive and his disparate deed.

Brutus is a Roman of noble mold; his excellence in private life is evident in his consideration for the sleepy servant boy Lucius, as well as in his relations with his wife Portia. Stoically restrained in his affection for his wife, Brutus controls his grief when he tells Cassius of her death, self-inflicted through solicitude for him.

Brutus' death, unlike that of Othello, is not associated with surrender to passion. His one outburst of passion appears momentarily in the quarrel with Cassius, when Brutus, unwilling to exact bribes, seeks unreasonably to profit from those exacted by Cassius. Cassius, perceiving the futility of argument, blames himself for the provocation of the quarrel and ultimately excuses Brutus because the outburst occurred just after Portia's death (of which Cassius was later informed).

It is on the battlefield that Brutus makes a great mistake so far as his personal safety is concerned: he gives disastrously faulty commands to the army. Cassius' surrender to Brutus in the quarrel and his subsequent yielding to

Brutus' argument to meet the enemy at Philippi is followed by Brutus' error in military judgment—an error which brings about the final catastrophe. Perceiving his own advantage over Octavius and unmindful of Cassius, Brutus orders his men to charge too early. The result is the supposed enclosure of Cassius' troops by Antony's and the suicide of Cassius, who thinks the battle over. Antony, thus conquering Cassius, is agent of revenge for the ghost of Caesar, as Cassius acknowledges before his suicide:

> *Caesar, thou art reveng'd,*
> *Even with the sword that kill'd thee.*

Cassius falls by the sword with which he stabbed Caesar, as Aeschylus' Clytemnestra and Aegisthus died by the axe which struck Agamemnon.

Brutus also recognizes Caesar's vengeance as fulfilled:

> *O Julius Caesar, thou are mighty yet!*
> *Thy spirit walks abroad, and turns our swords*
> *In our own proper entrails.*

But Brutus, the paragon of stoic virtue, a Roman who has schooled himself in renunciation, consoles himself:

> *I shall have glory by this losing day*
> *More than Octavius and Mark Antony*
> *By this vile conquest shall attain unto.*

In spite of the failure of his cause, Brutus is assured of the nobility of his action. Brutus' has not been a political or a military victory but a victory over himself. He has attained a virtue which is a state of mind impregnable to the blows of circumstance. In his character he finds consolation. Through adversity, which gives him opportunity to acquire indifference, he comes to the point at which, in a final act of fortitude, he can renounce life with the declaration

> ... *my bones would rest,*
> *That have but labour'd to attain this hour.*

Viewing life as a bondage, the Stoic can look upon his acquisition of fortitude culminating in suicide as did Brutus' servant Strato, who held the sword upon which his master ran:

> *For Brutus only overcame himself,*
> *And no man else hath honour by his death.*

Regarded from the stoic viewpoint, Brutus has no tragic fault. To the moment of his death, he has displayed nobility of character in actions which he never concedes to be wrong because they are made with good intention.[11] Hence the enemy Antony can pronounce appropriate eulogy over the body of the stoic hero:

> *This was the noblest Roman of them all.*
> *All the conspirators, save only he,*
> *Did that they did in envy of great Caesar;*
> *He only, in a general honest thought*
> *And common good to all, made one of them.*
> *His life was gentle, and the elements*
> *So mix'd in him that Nature might stand up*
> *And say to all the world, "This was a man!"*

NOTES

QUOTATIONS from the Greek and Roman tragedies and from Aristotle's *Nicomachean Ethics* are taken from the Loeb Classical Library translations, published by Harvard University Press. Quotations from Aristotle's *Poetics* and from Shakespeare's tragedies are taken from the following sources:

ARISTOTLE. *Aristotle's Theory of Poetry and Fine Art*, ed. S. H. Butcher (4th ed.). New York 19: Dover Publications, Inc., 1951. $4.50.

SHAKESPEARE. *The Complete Plays and Poems of William Shakespeare*, ed. William Allan Neilson and Charles Jarvis Hill (New Cambridge Edition). Boston: Houghton Mifflin Co., c. 1942.

CHAPTER ONE

1. Aristotle, *Poetics*, 1449a14-15.
2. John Dryden, *Works*, ed. George Saintsbury and Sir Walter Scott (London: William Paterson & Co., 1892), XV, 390.
3. S. H. Butcher, *Aristotle's Theory of Poetry and Fine Art*, 4th ed. (New York: Dover Publications, Inc., 1951), p. 302.
4. *Poetics*, 1450a37-38.
5. S. M. Pitcher, "The *Anthus* of Agathon," *American Journal of Philology*, LX (1939), 159.
6. *Poetics*, 1450a23-24.
7. *Ibid.*, 1454a16-19.
8. E. E. Stoll, *From Shakespeare to Joyce* (Garden City, N.Y.: Doubleday, Doran & Co., 1944), p. 288. Stoll comments that both the "Hellenic poets" and Shakespeare emphasize the element of goodness in the tragic hero. See also S. M. Pitcher, "Aristotle's Good and Just Heroes," *Philological Quarterly*, XXIV (1945), 1-11. It might be noted, however, that the word "hero" does not appear in the *Poetics*; see Lane Cooper, *Aristotelian Papers* (Ithaca, N.Y.: Cornell University Press, 1939), p. 82.
9. Aristotle, *Nicomachean Ethics*, 1106b27-1107a7.
10. *Ibid.*, 1109b14-23.
11. *Ibid.*, 1107a8-13.
12. E. E. Stoll, *Shakespeare Studies* (New York: The Macmillan Co.,

1927), pp. 102-103; *Shakespeare and Other Masters* (Cambridge: Harvard University Press, 1940), p. 27.
13. The self-descriptive method in its relation to the development of dramatic technique is discussed by Stoll in *Shakespeare Studies,* pp. 362-366.
14. W. C. Greene, *Moira: Fate, Good, and Evil in Greek Thought* (Cambridge: Harvard University Press, 1944), p. 8.

CHAPTER TWO

1. *Poetics,* 1453a30-39.
2. Greene, *Moira,* p. 322.
3. *Poetics,* 1453a30-39.
4. Allardyce Nicoll, *Introduction to Dramatic Theory* (London: George G. Harrap & Co., Ltd., 1923), p. 153. Nicoll discovers that Aristotle advances this view not only in the *Poetics* but also in the *Nicomachean Ethics.*
5. Alan Reynolds Thompson, *The Dry Mock: A Study of Irony in Drama* (Berkeley: University of California Press, 1948), p. 135. For a penetrating study of "Irony as Dramatic Emphasis: The Clytemnestra Plays," see G. G. Sedgewick's *Of Irony: Especially in Drama* (Toronto: University of Toronto Press, 1948), pp. 59-83.
6. C. R. Post, "The Dramatic Art of Sophocles," *Harvard Studies in Classical Philology,* XXIII (1912), 2.
7. Greene, *Moira,* p. 98.
8. *Ibid.,* p. 126. See also *Agamemnon,* 340.
9. S. H. Butcher, *Some Aspects of the Greek Genius* (London: Macmillan & Co., Ltd., 1929), pp. 108-111.
10. B. A. G. Fuller, "The Conflict of Moral Obligation in the Trilogy of Aeschylus," *Harvard Theological Review,* VIII (1915), 461. See also Greene, *Moira,* p. 125.
11. Greene, *Moira,* p. 91.
12. Sedgewick (p. 65) observes, "Indeed, a wave of ironic power is set moving in the first speech of the guard, gathers force as we watch Clytemnestra making her ominous preparations, mounts high with the pompous entrance of Agamemnon's chariot and Cassandra's, breaks terrifically in the clash between husband and wife; and then, with accelerated motion, a second wave lifts as Cassandra gathers together her divinations in the hearing of a frightened but ignorant chorus, and it too breaks with the scream of Agamemnon stricken."

13. G. D. Thomson (*The Oresteia of Aeschylus* [Cambridge: Cambridge University Press, 1938], I, 35-41) discusses the analogy between music and the trilogy.
14. Greene, *Moira*, p. 134.
15. *Ibid.*
16. Thomson (I, 49-53) develops the sociological import of the Aeschylean trilogy.
17. H. W. Smyth, *Aeschylean Tragedy* (Berkeley: University of California Press, 1924), p. 233. See also Aristotle, *Rhetoric*, 1374a11-14, 1374b.
18. *Nicomachean Ethics*, 1145b21-1152a36, 1144b26-30.
19. *Ibid.*, 1114a4-21; Greene, *Moira*, p. 327.
20. Stoll (*Shakespeare Studies*, pp. 351-354) discusses the significance of remorse and repentance with reference to Macbeth and various villains.

CHAPTER THREE

1. Greene, *Moira*, p. 141.
2. Thompson, *The Dry Mock*, p. 141.
3. *Ibid.*, p. 142.
4. *Ibid.*, p. 141.
5. *Ibid.*, pp. 29-31. Thompson (pp. 143-148) presents a digest of Thirlwall's essay "On the Irony of Sophocles," published in 1833 and giving a new application to the word *irony*.
6. Sedgewick, *Of Irony*, p. 59.
7. *Ibid.*
8. David Worcester, *The Art of Satire* (Cambridge: Harvard University Press, 1940), pp. 75-76.
9. Sedgewick, p. 63.
10. Pitcher, "Aristotle's Good and Just Heroes," 1-11.
11. Greene, *Moira*, p. 98.
12. *Ibid.*, p. 107.
13. *Ibid.*, p. 101.
14. Such is not the case with Aeschylus. Aeschylus consistently justifies the divine order, with the result that supernatural improbabilities are operative in the plot. They appeared in Aeschylus' trilogy, the *Oedipodeia* (of which only the second play, *The Seven Against Thebes*, is extant). Aeschylus tells a tale of inherited guilt and retribution, originating in the primal sin of the father of Oedipus, Laius. Laius, in retaliation for carrying off Pelops' son Chrysippus, brought on himself the curse of Pelops

reinforced by the triple warning of Apollo, who forbade him to beget a son. Laius ignored the warning and begot Oedipus, who in time slew his father and married his mother. Greene discusses Aeschylus' treatment of the Oedipus story in *Moira*, pp. 114-116.

15. H. D. F. Kitto, *Greek Tragedy* (London: Methuen & Co., Ltd., 1939), p. 105.

16. W. C. Greene, "The Murderers of Laius," *Transactions of the American Philological Association*, LX (1929), 75-85.

17. J. T. Sheppard (*The Oedipus Tyrannus of Sophocles* [Cambridge: Cambridge University Press, 1920]) makes this observation in the introduction to his translation (pp. 159-160).

18. ἅλις νουσοῦσ' ἐγώ.

19. A. E. Haigh (*The Tragic Drama of the Greeks* [Oxford: Clarendon Press, reprinted 1925], p. 176) analyzes the unconscious irony of Sophocles.

20. Sedgewick (pp. 39-44) gives examples from *Oedipus the King* and from *Othello* which produce the ironic effect without using "double-edged" speech.

21. G. R. Elliott, "*Othello* as a Love-Tragedy," *American Review*, VIII (1937), 274-275.

22. *Ibid.*, 267.

23. *Ibid.*, 274-275.

24. Sedgewick (p. 108) remarks in his chapter on "Irony as Dramatic Preparation" that "the bodyguard whom Othello trusted in Venice has won the complete confidence of Desdemona. He has fooled her, as he has fooled Roderigo, Brabantio, the Moor, and as he will fool Cassio presently. Everybody on the stage, so we see, has every reason to trust him implicitly—every reason, that is, *except the knowledge which only the spectator has.*"

25. Elliott, 260-265.

26. Fredson Thayer Bowers, *Elizabethan Revenge Tragedy (1587-1642)*, (Princeton: Princeton University Press, 1940), p. 49. Bowers discovers that "the Renaissance spirit of vengeance on an erring wife was not so much sexual jealousy (although this is a broad statement) as the desire to spoil the triumphs of others, and to vindicate oneself publicly. Where the wife's infidelities exposed the Italian husband to the derision of outsiders he was justified by public opinion, and condoned by the law, in resorting to murder." It should be observed that, though Shakespeare's Othello at one stage of the course of his vengeance seeks to "spoil the triumphs of others," Shakespeare does not here follow the Italian tradition in condoning Othello's act.

27. Sedgewick, pp. 87-114.

28. Kitto, p. 401.

29. On reconciliation in Sophoclean and Shakespearean tragedy, see Stoll, *Shakespeare and Other Masters*, pp. 59-84, 399.

30. S. T. Coleridge, *Coleridge's Shakespearean Criticism*, ed. Thomas Middleton Raysor (Cambridge: Harvard University Press, 1930), I, 59. See also Stoll, *Shakespeare and Other Masters*, p. 16.

31. Robert B. Heilman (*This Great Stage: Image and Structure in King Lear* [Baton Rouge: Louisiana State University Press, 1948], pp. 70-79) analyzes the clothes pattern and observes, "The clothes pattern makes a running commentary on the intellectual and moral problems that arise in Lear's kingdom."

32. R. C. Jebb, *Sophocles: the Plays and Fragments*, 2nd ed., Part III: *The Antigone* (Cambridge: Cambridge University Press, 1891), pp. xxvii-xxviii.

33. *Ibid.*, pp. xxviii-xxix.

34. *Ibid.*, pp. xiv-xv.

35. *Ibid.*, p. xxx. Stoll (*Shakespeare Studies*, p. 110) compares the minor importance of the Hamlet-Ophelia and the Antigone-Haemon love themes.

36. Philip Whaley Harsh (*A Handbook of Classical Drama* [Stanford: Stanford University Press, 1944], p. 107) observes the humorous nature of the guard's remarks.

37. Jebb, pp. xxxvi-xxxvii.

38. *Ibid.*, pp. xv-xvi.

39. *Ibid.*, p. xiii.

40. *Ibid.*, p. xxxii.

41. *Ibid.*, pp. xviii-xx. Stoll (*Shakespeare and Other Masters*, p. 72) compares Creon's delay in rescuing Antigone with Edgar's tardiness in rescuing Cordelia. Stoll contends that by the delay an anticlimax is averted in both cases.

42. E. E. Stoll, "*Hamlet*: an Historical and Comparative Study," *Research Publications of the University of Minnesota*, VIII (1919), 44.

43. E. E. Stoll, *Art and Artifice in Shakespeare*, p. 102.

44. *Ibid.*, pp. 128-129.

45. Greene, *Moira*, p. 101.

46. Greene, *Moira*, pp. 141-142. For a discussion of *arete* in relation to Sophocles and Euripides, see J. A. Moore, *Sophocles and Aretê* (Cambridge: Harvard University Press, 1938).

47. *Nicomachean Ethics*, 1100b30-33.

ETHICAL ASPECTS OF TRAGEDY

CHAPTER FOUR

1. *Poetics,* 1453a30.
2. Greene, *Moira,* p. 101.
3. Butcher, *Aristotle's Theory of Poetry and Fine Art,* pp. 264-265.
4. *Poetics,* 1460b34.
5. Greene, *Moira,* p. 217.
6. L. E. Matthaei, *Studies in Greek Tragedy* (Cambridge: Cambridge University Press, 1918), p. 80.
7. This fact Matthaei observes in her study (*ibid.,* p. 89).
8. Greene, *Moira,* pp. 181, 183.
9. Matthaei, p. 113.
10. E. E. Stoll, *Shakespeare's Young Lovers* (New York: Oxford University Press, 1937), p. 40.
11. On the traditional stage nurse see Kitto, *Greek Tragedy,* pp. 85-86, and H. B. Charlton, "*Romeo and Juliet* as an Experimental Tragedy," *Proceedings of the British Academy,* Vol. XXV London: Oxford University Press, 1939), p. 149.

CHAPTER FIVE

1. Thompson, *The Dry Mock,* pp. 63-64. Also Worcester, *The Art of Satire,* pp. 125-126.
2. Sedgewick, *Of Irony,* p. 15.
3. Haakon M. Chevalier, *The Ironic Temper: Anatole France and His Time* (New York: Oxford University Press, 1932), p. 79.
4. Thompson, p. 173.
5. A. R. Bellinger ("*The Bacchae* and *Hippolytus,*" *Yale Classical Studies,* Vol. VI [New Haven: Yale University Press, 1939], pp. 25-27) analyzes the *Bacchae* and compares the tragedy with *Hippolytus* "to show that its inconsistency has at least a technical explanation." The author finds a number of similarities: (1) between the characters of Hippolytus and of Pentheus; (2) between the deities Aphrodite and Dionysus; (3) in the shift in audience-sympathy for the leading characters; (4) in the manner of death of Hippolytus and of Pentheus; (5) in the suffering of Theseus and of Agave, who in ignorance destroy their children and admit their guilt to an outraged god.
6. W. B. Sedgwick ("Again the *Bacchae,*" *Classical Review,* XLIV [February, 1930], 6-8) considers Pentheus a typical Aristotelian hero—a good man who meets his downfall through *hamartia,* as the result of a traditional act of *hybris.* However, the fact that the god himself brings about the punishment instead of employ-

NOTES

ing human agencies raises problems of interpretation. The author
further observes that the myth itself was intended to glorify
Dionysus, and Euripides took the story as he found it—an observation which explains the origin of the plot but not its
ambiguity.

7. "The heart of the trouble is in the difficulty of determining
Euripides' attitude toward Dionysus. Is the God the real hero
of the play? In that case Pentheus is the villain, his overthrow
is the righteous triumph of insulted godhead, and the play is a
piece of thorough orthodoxy. Or, on the other hand, is Pentheus
the hero? Then he falls before superior force, not superior right;
Dionysus becomes a malevolent deity, and the play is a piece of
iconoclasm." Bellinger, pp. 17, 24.

8. Greene, *Moira*, p. 212.

9. "In theology the religion of Dionysus asserted the affinity and
possible union of the divine and the human nature; Dionysus
was of both natures; he proceeded from the supreme Deity
(Zeus) by a double generation; he was born first as man from
the body of a woman, and secondly as god from the body of
the Deity himself. The practice and ritual consisted, so far as
was essential and peculiar, totally in the cultivation and stimula-
tion of the divine element in man by the voluntary production
of ecstasy." A. W. Verrall, *The Bacchants of Euripides and
Other Essays* (Cambridge: Cambridge University Press, 1910),
p. 2.

R. B. Appleton (*Euripides: The Idealist* [New York: E. P.
Dutton & Co., 1927], pp. 181-182), after reminding his readers
that the slaying and dismembering of Pentheus is not part of the
Bacchic rites but an act of divine vengeance, calls attention to
the fact that Dionysus was not an original member of the Olympian hierarchy but a comparatively late comer who seemed to be
welcomed as a new god who could give life to "the outworn
creed of Olympian theology."

10. Bellinger, pp. 25, 21.

11. Kitto (*Greek Tragedy*, pp. 374-386 *passim*) likens the presumption of Pentheus here symbolically displayed to the presumption
of Aeschylus' Agamemnon and its symbolic representation in the
purple carpet. Kitto also discusses the theory of Verrall and
Norwood (with regard to the "palace-miracle") that the god of
the prologue and the priest of the rest of the tragedy are two
different persons. Verrall insists that Dionysus' words mean that
the palace is utterly destroyed, but since it is not—for later

Pentheus and his enemy enter the palace before proceeding to Cithaeron—Dionysus is no god but an impostor.

12. Greene, *Moira*, p. 176.

13. G. M. A. Grube ("Dionysus in the *Bacchae*," *Transactions and Proceedings of the American Philological Association*, LXVI [1935], 37-54) discussing the part of Dionysus, shows the effect of Euripides' "whitewashing" of Pentheus in diminishing, by contrast, the audience-sympathy for the god. "The lament of Cadmus over his grandson and only heir incidentally shows Pentheus, whom we have only seen in a towering rage, in a more human light, giving protection to the old man against all comers, and though the full kingly power had been surrendered to him, he did not, it seems, forget the man from whom it came. The whitewashing of the villain, be it only posthumously, is almost a commonplace of Euripides' dramatic technique. It was continued, if we may believe the authorities, in the lament of Agave which is now lost, and she too enlisted our sympathy, which Dionysus has forfeited, on the side of her dead son."

14. Bellinger (pp. 23-24) discusses the possibilities of that part of the drama which is missing..

15. M. W. MacCallum, *Shakespeare's Roman Plays* (London: Macmillan and Co., Ltd., 1925), pp. 397-399.

16. Harley Granville-Barker, *Prefaces to Shakespeare* (London: Sidgwick and Jackson, Ltd., 1935), pp. 224-227.

17. E. E. Stoll, *Poets and Playwrights* (Minneapolis: University of Minnesota Press, 1930), p. 26.

18. MacCallum (p. 342) compares the love themes of three of Shakespeare's tragedies. "In *Romeo and Juliet* he idealises youthful love with its raptures, its wonders, its overthrow in collision with the harsh facts of life. *Troilus and Cressida* shows the inward dissolution of such love when it is unworthily bestowed, and suffers from want of reverence and loftiness. In *Antony and Cleopatra* love is not a revelation as in the first, nor an illusion as in the second, but an infatuation. There is nothing youthful about it, whether as adoration or inexperience. It is the love that seizes the elderly man of the world, the trained mistress of arts, and does this, as it would seem, to cajole and destroy them both."

19. *Ibid.*, pp. 450-451. Of Cleopatra MacCallum remarks: "And her love, too, though perhaps more fitfully, yet all the more strikingly, is deepened and solemnised by trial. After Actium it quite loses its element of mockery and petulance. Her flout at Antony's negligence before the battle is the last we hear her utter. Henceforth,

whether she protests her faith, or speeds him to the fight, or welcomes him on his return, her words have a new seriousness and weight."

20. *Ibid.*, p. 451: "The most wonderful touch of all is that now she feels her right to be considered his wife."

21. *Ibid.*, p. 341: "To him Antony's devotion to Cleopatra is the grand fact in his career, which bears witness to his greatness as well as to his littleness, and is at once his perdition and his apotheosis."

22. Dryden comments in his Preface to *All for Love*: "All reasonable men have long since concluded, That the Heroe of the Poem ought not to be a character of perfect Virtue, for, then, he could not without injustice, be made unhappy; nor yet altogether wicked, because he could not then be pitied: I have therefore steer'd the middle course, and have drawn the character of *Antony* as favourably as *Plutarch*, *Appian*, and *Dion Cassius* wou'd give me leave; the like I have observ'd in *Cleopatra*: That which is wanting to work up the pity to a greater heighth was not afforded me by the story; for the crimes of love which they both committed, were not occasion'd by any necessity, or fatal ignorance, but were wholly voluntary; since our passions are, or ought to be, within our power." *Dramatic Works*, ed. Montague Summers (London: Nonesuch Press, 1932), IV, 180-181.

CHAPTER SIX

1. Willard Farnham, *The Medieval Heritage of Elizabethan Tragedy* (Berkeley: University of California Press, 1936), pp. 419-420.

2. Greene, *Moira*, p. 142. The Greek word *arete* connotes the Latin word *virtus*.

3. *Ibid.*, p. 341.

4. *Ibid.*, p. 342.

5. *Ibid.*, p. 161.

6. Farnham, p. 18.

7. Hardin Craig ("The Shackling of Accidents: A Study of Elizabethan Tragedy," *Philological Quarterly*, XIX [1940], 1-19 *passim*) develops the general idea of stoic fortitude with reference to Seneca's Hercules.

8. Bowers (*Elizabethan Revenge Tragedy*, p. 264) finds that "Atreus, Aegisthus, and Medea—Seneca's three great revengers—are all villains, and Deïanira of *Hercules Oetaeus*, who is a revenger in error, is cleared of her crime by an expiatory suicide."

9. Greene, *Moira*, p. 423.
10. Farnham, p. 20.
11. Farnham (pp. 418-419) comments: "Shakespeare's Brutus asks admission to the ranks of those creatures of poesy who work out some tragic destiny in the grand manner of profound irony, not as pawns of Fortune or the gods, nor as magnificently defiant sinners, nor as headstrong weaklings, but as men of heroic strength of goodness whose admirable qualities lead them into suffering. They are often forced to take the wages of what has the appearance of evil action and yet is not to be called evil action in all simplicity because it is dictated by their nobility."

INDEX

Aegisthus, 11, 19, 20, 24, 115
Aeschylus, 8-9, 10-26 *passim*, 28, 31, 34-36, 43-44, 55, 69, 76-77, 84, 88, 102-103, 115; *Agamemnon*, 8, 10-21; *Eumenides*, 9, 24-26; *Libation-Bearers*, 21-24; *Oresteia*, 9, 10-26, 35, 69, 76; *Prometheia*, 9
Agamemnon, 11-21, 24, 26, 31, 43, 113, 115
Agathon, 3
Agave, 91, 94-95
Alastor, 9, 19-20
Anthus, 3
Antigone, 46, 55, 59, 64-68, 73
Antony, 6, 95-101, 113, 115-116
Aphrodite, 77-79, 81-84, 89, 91
Apollo, 14, 22-26, 36-37, 39, 45, 55, 84
Areopagus, 25-26
Arete (*see also* Virtue), 74, 103-104
Aristotle, 1, 9, 27-28, 31-34, 45, 55, 59-60, 74-76, 88, 102-103, 109; *Nicomachean Ethics*, 2; *Poetics*, 1-3, 8, 45; *Rhetoric*, 2
Artemis, 6, 13, 78-79, 81-84, 87, 89-90
Athena, 25-26

Banquo, 27, 29-30
Brutus, 6, 99, 103, 111-115
Butcher, S. H., 2, 76

Caesar, Julius, 96, 111-116

Caesar, Octavius, 97-101, 113, 115
Cassandra, 14, 16, 18, 20, 24
Cassio, 6, 48-49, 53-54
Cassius, 112-115
Chance, 15
Chastity (*see also* Honesty), 49, 79, 81-82, 85, 89, 92
Chevalier, H. M., 88
Chorus, tragic, 5-6, 13, 97
Christianity, 5, 8, 28, 111
Claudius, 68, 70-71
Cleopatra, 95-101
Clytemnestra, 6, 8-9, 11, 13-24, 26, 28-29, 31, 115
Coleridge, S. T., 59
Comedy, 9, 33
Conscience, 28-31
Cordelia, 59-63
Cosmos, 33, 78
Creon, 38-40, 46, 55-56, 64-68, 70, 73
Curse, 12, 14-15, 18-21, 24, 35, 38, 41, 56-57, 60, 64-65, 68, 82

Degeneration, 8-9, 27
Deianira, 105, 107, 109
De Providentia, 110
Desdemona, 49-54, 61
Dionysus, 77, 89-96, 98
Dreams, 21-22, 24, 85
Dryden, 1, 101

Electra, 21-22
Enobarbus, 97-99, 101
Erinyes (*see also* Eumenides), 23-26

127

Eteocles, 57, 64
"*Ethos*," 1-7 *passim*, 32-34, 37, 75, 88-89, 102
Eumenides (*see also* Erinyes), 26, 57
Euripides, 1, 10, 75-84 *passim*, 87, 89-95 *passim*, 104-105, 108; *Bacchae*, 77, 88-96; *Hippolytus*, 75-84, 87, 89
Expiation, 45

Fate, 25-26, 33, 35, 47, 74, 84-85, 108
Fault (*see also* Flaw; *Hamartia*; Sin), 3, 47, 61, 83, 85, 87, 103, 109, 113, 116
Flaw (*see also* Fault; *Hamartia*; Sin), 3, 32
Forgiveness, 70, 81, 84, 87, 107
Fortune, 32, 43, 85-86

Ghosts, 21, 29, 69, 72, 115
Greene, W. C., 35, 73, 78, 110

Haemon, 66-68, 71
Hamartia (*see also* Fault; Flaw; Sin), 3, 5, 32
Hamlet, 6, 68-73
Hamlet, elder, 70, 72-73
Helen, 13
Hercules, 103, 105-109, 111, 114
Hippolytus, 6, 78-85, 87, 89-90, 95
Homer, *Odyssey*, 11
Honesty (*see also* Chastity), 48-49
Horace, 3
Hybris, 4, 12-14, 17-19, 31, 40, 43, 68, 93

Iago, 6, 48-50, 52, 54

Improbabilities, dramatic, 36, 59-60
Iphigenia, 12-14, 20, 24
Irony, 9, 24, 32-33, 35, 43, 45, 47, 49, 55, 72, 75, 77, 82, 84, 88, 113; "Poetic Irony," 32-34, 59; "Romantic Irony," 88-89
Ius naturale; Ius civile, 26

Jocasta, 37, 40-44, 80
Juliet, 61, 84-87
Justice, 9, 17, 20, 24, 26, 31-32, 34, 36, 53-54, 63, 73, 77, 84, 90, 113; "Poetic Justice," 8-9, 31-32, 90

Katharsis, 2, 76
Kent, 60-61, 63

Laius, 36-39, 41-42, 44
Lear, 6, 59-63

Macbeth, 8-9, 27-31
Macbeth, Lady, 27-30
Macduff, 29, 31
Mean, doctrine of the, 4
Motives, 20, 22-26, 37, 55, 74, 99, 102-104, 109, 114

Nemesis (*see also* Retribution; Vengeance), 4, 12, 17-18, 29, 43, 93
Nero, 103, 110-111
Nicoll, A., 9
Nurse, 23, 78-80, 83, 86, 106-107

Oaths, 80, 83
Oedipus, 6, 32-33, 36-48, 55-59, 63-64, 104, 108, 113
Ophelia, 71
Oracles (*see also* Prophecy), 32, 37, 39-40, 42, 47, 55-57, 108

Orestes, 8, 11, 18, 21-27, 44-45, 84, 113

Othello, 6, 47-54, 114

"Pathos," 30, 53, 75-76, 84, 87

Pentheus, 77, 89-96, 98

Phaedra, 77-84, 89, 108

Piety, 84, 92

Plato, 102

Pleasure, tragic, 2, 5

Plutarch, 97, 101, 111

Polis (*see also* State), 102

Pollution, 24, 37-39, 41, 44, 67

Polyneices, 57, 60, 64-65, 68, 73

Pompey, 97-98, 112

Prometheus, 9

Prophecy (*see also* Oracles), 40, 42, 47, 94

Prosperity, 43

Providence, 73

Punishment, 9, 34-35, 66, 77, 94, 108

Purification, 25

Reason, 26, 38-40, 47, 65, 71, 77, 83, 92, 96, 102, 104, 111-112

Recognition, tragic, 33, 44

Reconciliation, 55, 87

Renunciation, 107, 110-111, 115

Reputation, 37, 49, 54, 72, 80, 83, 89, 91, 100

Retribution (*see also* Nemesis; Vengeance), 12, 67, 71, 104

Revenge, 69-70, 72, 78, 115

Reversal, tragic, 33, 42-43

Romeo, 84-87

Schlegel, F., 88

Sedgewick, G. G., 33, 88

Semele, 90-91

Seneca, 6, 70, 102-111 *passim*,

114; *Hercules Furens,* 110; *Hercules Oetaeus,* 103-111

Shakespeare, 2, 3, 5-6, 10, 27-31 *passim,* 46-55 *passim,* 58-63 *passim,* 68-74 *passim,* 75, 84-87 *passim,* 95-101 *passim,* 103, 111-116 *passim; Antony and Cleopatra,* 89, 95-101; *Hamlet,* 68-74; *Julius Caesar,* 103, 111-116; *King Lear,* 58-63; *Macbeth,* 6, 9, 27-31; *Othello,* 46-55; *Romeo and Juliet,* 75, 84-87

Sin (*see also* Fault; Flaw; *Hamartia*), 4, 28, 35, 87

Skepticism, 77

Socrates, 102

Sophocles, 1-2, 10, 12, 32-46 *passim,* 54-58 *passim,* 64-68 *passim,* 75-77, 80, 82, 88, 102-104, 108; *Antigone,* 64-68, 70-72; *Oedipus at Colonus,* 36, 45-46, 55-59, 63-64, 77; *Oedipus the King,* 34-46, 54-57, 59

Sophrosyne, 46

Sphinx, 37, 39

State (*see also Polis*), 37-38, 40, 47, 54, 63, 65, 67, 71, 73, 102, 113-114

"Stoicism," 99, 102-103, 111

Suicide, 54, 68, 80, 100, 107-108, 110, 114-116

Sympathy, 2, 18, 23-24, 31, 57, 62, 71, 80, 90, 94-95, 108-109, 113

Teiresias, 6, 39-40, 66-67, 71, 92-94

Theseus, 56-58, 77, 80-83

Thompson, A. R., 9, 32-33, 88

Tieck, L., 88

Tragedy, idea of, 1, 34, 60, 76-77, 86

Utile dulci, 3

Vengeance (see also Nemesis; Retribution), 9, 12, 21-22, 26, 80, 95, 106, 115

Vindication, 32, 53, 58, 68, 73, 82-83

Virtue (see also Arete), 4, 104-105, 111, 115

Will, 12, 15, 27-28, 39, 44, 58, 68, 74, 83-84, 102, 104-105

Wisdom, 14, 36, 68, 102-103

Worcester, D., 33

Zeus, 9-10, 13-15, 19, 25-26, 34, 36-37, 43, 90, 94

DATE DUE

JAN 2 2 1979		
DEC 1 7 1979		
FEB 2 5 1986		
30 505 JOSTEN'S			,3